DIVORCE

A GIFT OF GOD'S LOVE

DIVORCE
A GIFT OF GOD'S LOVE

Walter L. Callison

A division of Squire Publishers, Inc.
4500 College Blvd.
Leawood, KS 66211
1/888/888-7696

ISBN: 1-58597-144-8

Library of Congress Control Number: 2002106809

A division of Squire Publishers, Inc.
4500 College Blvd.
Leawood, KS 66211
1/888/888-7696

DIVORCE CHANGE REQUESTED

NEW YORK — In a study of religiously observant Jewish women in broken marriages, Benita Gayle-Almeleh of the American Jewish Committee, has urged rabbinical action to remedy the paradoxical plight of thousands of Jewish women unable to obtain a religious divorce.

"She's in a limbo, neither married, nor unmarried," said Gayle-Almeleh of Jewish women divorced by civil action, but whose civilly divorced husbands won't grant a religious bill of divorcement called a *get*.

According to Jewish law as observed in Conservative and Orthodox Judaism, only the man can grant a *get*.

If he refuses, the woman's marriage, though ended civilly, is still binding religiously.

In such circumstances, said Gayle-Almeleh, a woman is "not free to remarry, to pick up the pieces and go on with her life."

Gayle-Almeleh estimates at least 35,000 Jewish women across the country are trapped in that situation (Wichita Beacon, Wichita, Ks., 2-20-'88).

MALACHI 2:16

For the Lord, the God of Israel, saith that he hateth *putting away:* for one covereth violence with his garment, saith the Lord of hosts: therefore take heed to your spirit, that ye deal not treacherously (italics mine).

TABLE OF CONTENTS

PREFACE i

PROLOGUE: Divorce, the Law, and Jesus — from *Your Church* magazine, May-June 1986, by Walter L. Callison
> Requests for more material from readers of this article were overwhelming, and provided major motivation for this book.

Chapter

1. "For the Hardness of Your Heart" 11

2. The Struggle for Control 19

3. Justification by Tradition 25

4. The Crux of the Matter:

   "I hate putting away, saith Jehovah" 31

5. And Jesus Came 41

6. Why Wasn't It Corrected? 47

7. Adultery and the Sanctity of Marriage 55

8. "If It Is a Girl, Throw It Away" 65

9. "Pioneers of the New Humanity" 69

10. Who Made You My Judge? 75

11. How Serious Is Divorce? 83

12. What About It, Paul? 93

13. Divorce Is Not the Problem 99

14. Going On 105

PREFACE

DIVORCE, a gift of God's love. Yes, a gift of God's love!

After a 25-year struggle with the content as well as the title of this study, a dear lady in Texas convinced me that her divorce was, indeed, a gift from God. Her church didn't see it that way. Neither does mine. Yours probably does not, either.

This study is an outgrowth of an article I wrote entitled, "Divorce, the Law, and Jesus." Publication of the article brought about a staggering number of requests for more information.

As I struggled with a title for this larger work I tried a number of them, but could not settle on one. More or less in desperation, I affixed the title of the article, "Divorce, the Law, and Jesus." I was never satisfied that it really expressed anything of my convictions about the subject.

An opportunity first came to share my study with the husband of the lady mentioned, an educator friend, and retired in Edinburg, Texas. He was totally supportive of my endeavor and asked for permission to share it with his wife. His opinion was that no human should ever have to endure what she had from her church both before and after her divorce.

She knew our record. With further encouragement from her husband, she looked at it, liked it, and became convinced, with her husband, that I needed a title that told the truth about the subject matter. After a nearly sleepless night I bounced the title, "Divorce, A Gift of God's Love" off them. It is honest. That is what God means it to be. They liked it.

Yes, you don't have to tell me that divorce is often misused and abused. So is the Bible, a most precious gift of God's love. I think we could make a general rule that the more precious the gift of God, the more serious is its misuse. We will discuss this matter of abuse and mis-use later on.

I didn't choose to have the past 25 years of my life so wrapped up in the study of divorce and re-marriage. Sometimes God simply put the matter before me in an unavoidable manner. The direction a Christian ministry takes is truly a matter of—"We live by faith, and not by sight." (2 Corinthians 5:7).

I am convinced that God is, always has been, and always will be the God of love, as most fully revealed in Jesus Christ. He was not a different sort of God in Old Testament days, though his reporters had not yet seen the fullness of him in Jesus Christ. "These were all commended for faith, yet none of them received what had been promised." "Jesus Christ is the same yesterday and today and forever." (Hebrews 11:39 and 13:8).

Neither my wife nor I have been divorced. We do, however, remember a young marine who came home from Okinawa, divorced while serving there; and a middle-aged pastor whose wife could no longer tolerate the restrictions imposed upon her by his career; and a husband who deserted his wife and children. We also have experienced the agony of reaching out to help divorced people in the name of Christ, only to find them afraid of us and the church from which we reached.

I dare to hope this study may provide some fresh insight into the problems our churches have ministering to the divorced, may even change some of our attitudes about those who have suffered this tragedy.

I have arrived at a point of view which is an extreme departure from the traditional, and which will certainly be controversial to some.

The case histories included are real, and many are too close to home for comfort; the names are not real. The experiences, which led me to this study, go back through over thirty-five years of Christian ministry and a twenty-year career in the United States Navy.

Though this study is based on an apparent mis-translation of a Greek word, you do not need any knowledge of the Hebrew or Greek languages to be able to understand what I have written. A reading of the gospel seems to reveal that anyone could serve Christ and would be accepted by him in person. Why cannot we in whom he dwells, his body, his church, be as he would be to all, including the divorced?

In preparing this study, I have used the following sources,

and acknowledge with gratitude, the aid I have received from them: *A Greek-English Lexicon,* Arndt-Gingrich; *The Life and Works of Josephus,* Whiston; *Langenscheidt Pocket Hebrew Dictionary,* Langenscheidt; *Analytical Hebrew and Chaldee Lexicon,* Benjamin Davidson; *Holy Bible,* American Standard Version; *Holy Bible,* King James Version; *The Greek New Testament,* United Bible Societies; *A Concise Greek-English Dictionary of the New Testament,* Newman; *Strong's Exhaustive Concordance,* Strong; *The New World,* Dana; *Holy Bible,* Revised Standard Version; *Introducing the Bible,* Barclay; *The Broadman Bible Commentary,* Stagg; *For This Day,* Phillips; *Wayward Bus,* Steinbeck; and *The New Testament, An Expanded Translation,* Wuest; *Holy Bible From The Ancient Eastern Text (George M. Lamsa's Translation From The Aramaic Of The Peshitta),* Lamsa; Malachi: *Rekindling The Fires Of Faith,* Kelley.

Portions of the content of this study have been published by the Missouri Baptist *Word and Way* in a three-part series entitled "The Bible Looks at Divorce," and by the *Your Church* magazine in an article entitled "Divorce, the Law, and Jesus."

My wife, Clarine, of 54 wonderful years; Dr. Ben Owen of Big Island, Virginia; Dr. Bill Coble of Midwestern Baptist Theological Seminary, Kansas City, Missouri; and Dr. Temp Sparkman of Midwestern Baptist Theological Seminary of Kansas City, Missouri have been of special help and encouragement to me. I would be remiss if I did not remember, also, the late Harvey Brown, as well as the congregation of the Cairo Baptist Church, Cairo, Missouri, and the University Baptist Church, Iowa City, Iowa, who were so kind and helpful as I worked through this matter as their pastor; and in these most recent days of struggle, Dr. and Mrs. Jim Robbins of Edinburg, Texas, and our constantly supportive and gracious daughter-in-law, Mrs. John (Linda) Callison of Joplin, Missouri. Thank you.

Special Note: Because most of our understanding about divorce and marriage has come to us from the wording of the King James Version of the Bible, it will be the basic text used in this study.

> Are people who are divorced and married to another living in adultery?
>
> How did we ever begin to read "whosoever divorces his wife" into those places where Jesus literally said "whosoever puts away or abandons his wife"?
>
> It is easy to preach against divorce, but difficult for a church to be constructive in providing preparation for marriage.

PROLOGUE

Divorce, the Law and Jesus

Reprinted from Your Church magazine of May-June 1986
YOUR CHURCH magazine, 198 Allendale Road, King of Prussia, PA 19406

"For the law was given by Moses, but grace and truth came by Jesus Christ (John 1:17)." Grace. Did grace come by Jesus Christ to those suffering marital tragedy, even as much grace as was provided by Old Testament law? Surely, we affirm, *grace and truth* did come by Jesus Christ. Then how does grace abound to those who have suffered the tragedy of a marriage failure and divorce?

Christ did more than teach with words. He also taught with his life. Christ brought new ideas to his followers, rejecting their ancient *"eye for an eye"* and *"tooth for a tooth"* doctrines, encouraging love for those not their own, lifting up women from the status of *"things"* to recognition as people. Yet he also taught respect for the old Jewish law.

When we study what he said about divorce, we must also study the life he lived among those of broken marriages, as well as what he taught about Jewish law, especially their divorce law.

But what about his words? If a divorced person is remarried, what about the words, *"Whosoever putteth away his, wife and marrieth another committeth adultery"* (Luke 16:18)? We could emulate the compassionate and forgiving nature of Christ, as he sent the woman at the well into Samaria to be his witness. But do his words deny his actions? Are people who are divorced and married to another living in adultery? Are they forbidden service to Christ?

We also must hear the words of the Apostle Paul. *"A bishop then must be blameless, the husband of one wife"* (I Tim. 3:2). Does he speak of a person who has been divorced and remarried?

Luke records only one comment, and a very concise one, on this subject:

"And it is easier for heaven and earth to. pass, than one tittle of the law to fail. Whosoever putteth away his wife, and marrieth another, committeth adultery; and whosoever marrieth her that is put away from her husband committeth adultery" (Luke 16:17-18).

Concise. But Jesus did make it clear that the Old Testament had something significant to say. There is a law! When asked by the Pharisees, in the Gospel of Mark, *"Is it lawful for a man to. put away his wife?"* (Mark 10:2), Jesus answered, *"What did Moses command you?"* (Mark 10:3). *"They said, Moses suffered to write a bill of divorcement"* (Mark 10:4). There is a law.

The law is found in Deuteronomy 24:1-4, and at the time Christ lived, Flavius Josephus, who also lived then, paraphrased it and referred to it as the *"law of the Jews"*:

"He that desires to be divorced from his wife for any cause whatsoever, (and many such causes happen among men), let him in writing give assurance that he will never use her as his wife any more; for by this means she may be at liberty to marry another husband, although before this bill of divorce be given, she is not to be permitted so to do..." **Antiquities of the Jews (The Life and Work of Flavius Josephus),** Book IV, Ch. VIII, Sec. 23, p. 134; (tr. Wm. Whiston; Holt, Rinehart, and Winston, NY).

Here is the law from Deuteronomy:

"When a man hath taken a wife, and married her, and it come to pass that she find no favour in his eyes, because he hath found some uncleanness in her: then let him write her a bill of divorcement, and give it in her hand, and send her out of his house. And when she is departed out of his house, she may go and be another man's wife" (Deut. 24:1.2).

The law was still around in the time of Christ. We must, therefore, deal with the *"tittles"* of the law. The Bible only records ONE divorce. **God said he did it.** In Jeremiah. 3, God reminded Judah that she was heading for trouble. Israel had already been taken captive. God told Jeremiah to warn Judah that she had witnessed her sister Israel's infidelity and had seen God give her a bill of divorce and send her away; and yet she did not fear (Jer. 3:6-8).

There were other things men did with their wives. Many men of old married more than one wife, and without bothering about divorce. Some of these were God's servants; Solomon, David, Abraham, and Esau, for example. Heroes of God's revelation, but also products of their culture.

If he did not divorce her, what did a man of those days do with a wife when he took another? He ***put her away.*** There is a word for that in the Old Testament, the Hebrew word "shalach." It is different than the Hebrew word for *"divorce,"* which is *"keriythuwth"* (Jer. 3:8 above) literally means excision, a cutting of the marital bonds; legal divorce was written, as commanded in Deuteronomy 24, and permitted subsequent marriage. *"Shalach"* is usually translated *"to put away."* Women were *"put away"* when their men married others, *put away* to be available if needed or wanted again, put away to become mere property, as slaves, or *put away* in total dismissal; it was a cruel day for women. They were *"put away"* in favor of another, but not given a divorce and the right to marry again. This word described a cruel tradition, common, but contrary to Jewish law.

Some of the hardships and terror experienced by women who were *"put away"* can be seen as this Hebrew word *"shalach"* is described in the ***Langenscheid Pocket Hebrew***

Dictionary (McGraw-Hill, 1969) *"to let loose, roaming at large, to be scared, abandoned, forsaken."*

J. B. Phillips, in his book of meditations For This Day (Word, 1975) wrote:

"The Christian faith took root and flourished in an atmosphere almost entirely pagan, where cruelty and sexual immorality were taken for granted, where slavery and the inferiority of women were almost universal, while superstition and rival religions with all kinds of bogus claims existed on every hand."

God hated this *"putting away."* Malachi, the prophet, broken-heartedly pleaded with God's people to stop the practice. Hear Malachi plead with them. The word translated *"putting away"* in Mal. 2:16 is not the Hebrew word for *"divorce"* but it is *"shalach,"* put away. Hear Malachi respond to leaders who asked how they had dealt treacherously, and committed abomination in Israel, and profaned the holiness of the Lord.

*"Yet ye say, Wherefore? Because the Lord hath been witness between thee and the wife of thy youth. against whom thou hast dealt treacherously: yet is she thy companion, and the wife of the covenant. And did not he make one? Yet had he the residue of the spirit. And wherefore one? That he might seek a godly seed. Therefore, take heed to your spirit, and let none deal treacherously against the wife of his youth. For the Lord, the God of Israel, saith that he hateth **putting away**"* (Mal. 2:14-16).

And Jesus came. And his words do not deny his actions! He spoke of this when he said, *"Whosoever putteth away his wife, and marrieth another, committeth adultery: and whosoever marrieth her that is put away from her husband committeth adultery"* (Luke 16:18). Whosoever does this commits adultery! This practice was cruel and was adulterous, but it was not divorce.

This New Testament word, translated *"put away"* in the King James Version, is a form of the Greek word *"apoluo."* It is the word in Greek, the language of the New Testament, which parallels the Hebrew word *"shalach" (put away).*

There is an Old Testament Hebrew word for divorce, *"keriythuwth,"* and a New Testament Greek word, apostasion. The **Arndt-Gingrich Lexicon of the New Testament** cites usage of the word apostasion for the technical term for a bill or writing of divorce as far back as 258 B.C.

"Apoluo," the Greek word for putting away, was not technically divorce, though often used synonymously. In that time of total male domination, men often took additional wives, and did not provide a written release when they forsook wives and married others. The Jewish law demanding written divorce (Deut. 24:1.2) was largely ignored. If a man married another woman, so what? If a man *"put away"* (apoluo) his wife without bothering with a written divorce, who was going to object? The woman?

Jesus had some objections. Jesus even loved mistreated women! He told them that this earth would go up in smoke before the law requiring a written bill of divorce should fail (Lk. 16:17). And he said, when you put away a wife (without written divorce), and marry another (while still married), you are guilty of adultery (Lk. 16:17). Moreover, she who is put away is in real trouble. She has no divorce paper. She is abandoned, but still married. She would commit adultery if she married again (Lk. 16:18).

The distinction between *"put away"* and *"divorce,"* between the Greek *"apoluo"* and *"apostasion"* is critical. *"Apoluo"* indicated that women were enslaved, put away, with no rights, no recourse; deprived of the basic right to monogamous marriage. *"Apostasion"* ended marriage and permitted a legal subsequent marriage. The paper makes a difference. *"Let him write her a bill of divorcement, and give it in her hand, and send her out of his house. And when she is departed out of his house, she may go and be another man's wife"* (Deut. 24:2). That was the law.

There are passages, other than Luke 16:17-18 (above) where Jesus spoke on this matter. They include Matt. 19:9, Mark 10:10-12 (where Mark records that Jesus laid down the same law for women as for men), and Matt. 5:32. Jesus used a form of the word *"apoluo"* eleven times in these passages. In every passage he forbade *apoluo, putting away*. He never forbade giving *"apostasion,"* written divorce, required by Jewish law.

Should the Greek word apoluo be translated *divorce?* Kenneth S. Wuest in **The New Testament, an Expanded Translation** always translated it *"dismissed"* or *"put away,"* never *"divorced."* The old, and very literal American Standard Version always translated it "put away." The **King James Version** translated it *"put away"* ten out of the eleven times Jesus used it. That eleventh instance seems to be the source of the problem. In 1611, in **ONE** place the **King James** translators wrote *"divorced"* instead of *"put away."* In Matt. 5:32, they wrote, *"and whosoever shall marry her that is divorced committeth adultery."* The word is not the Greek word *"apostasion"* (divorce), but is a form of that same Greek word *"apoluo,"* which did not include a writing of divorce for the woman. She, technically, would still be married.

Matt. 19:3-10 records the Pharisees taunting Jesus about this matter, asking him, *"Is it lawful for a man to put away his wife for every cause?"* He responded that marriage is a permanent relationship, and said, *"Whatsoever God hath joined together, let not man put asunder"* (Matt. 19:6).

They then asked, *"Why did Moses then command to give a writing of divorcement (apostasion), and to put her away?"* (Matt. 19:7); Jesus answered. *"because of the hardness of your hearts!"* (Matt, 19:8). The first basic human right God gave us was the right to be married. No other companionship is adequate. Hard-hearted men unilaterally put away women and married others, considering themselves divorced, but leaving the women without recourse and deprived of that first basic human right. Human rights were for men only in those days. Jesus changed that! He demanded obedience to the law; he demanded equal marriage rights for women. Grace does abound in Jesus Christ!

Jesus told those men that to put away a wife and to marry another was adultery. Adultery! The law (Deut. 22:22) called for the death penalty for adultery, for both the woman and the man! That was bitter medicine for the men who did as they pleased with women. Matt. 19:10 records their shock: *"If the case of a man be so with his wife, it is not good to marry."* They did not live in a culture wherein a man was expected to live with only one woman for life, much less, give her equal rights if marriage failed.

How did we ever begin to read *"whosoever divorces his wife"* into those places where Jesus literally said *"whosoever puts away, or abandons, his wife"?*

It may be that the one place where *apoluo* was mistranslated *"divorced"* in 1611 started the whole process. The **American Standard Version** corrected the error in 1901. It never became popular enough to make much difference. Wuest was careful to avoid such mistakes, as noted earlier. But almost every thing that has ever come off a printing press has been influenced by the **King James Version** of the Bible, even Greek English lexicons, and most modern translators seem to be influenced by that one occurrence in it and translate *"apoluo"* as *"divorce,"* even though the meaning of the word does not include a writing of divorce *(apostasion).* Now, tradition has taught us to record *"divorced"* in our minds, though our eyes actually read *"put away"* in the **King James Version.**

Is written divorce, as commanded in Deuteronomy, the solution to the cruel practice of *"putting away"?* The twenty-fourth chapter of Deuteronomy is evidence that, even as God heard the groaning of his people in Egypt and provided deliverance from slavery, he also heard the groans of enslaved women and provided deliverance from abuse by means of that tragic necessity, divorce; tragic because it ends that which should never end, marriage; necessary to protect the victims of those who do not obey the rules of our creator, all-mighty God. Necessary, originally, because men *"put away"* women, trapping them in illegal and adulterous multiple marriages. Divorce is a tragedy.

Divorce is a privilege, provided as a corrective for an intolerable situation. It is a privilege which can be, and often is, abused. Divorce is not a pretty picture in most cases. Loneliness, rejection, a deep sense of failure, loss of self-esteem, critical relatives, child care problems, property settlements — these concerns, and more confront the divorced.

Divorce can be more traumatic than the death of a mate. Grief following the death of a spouse is hard to bear, as is the grief of divorce. But a dead spouse does not keep coming back. The divorced one often does, thus prolonging and often renewing grief. Divorce is still only what it was in Jesus' day, a partial solution to a serious and cruel situation; and maybe the only reasonable solution. It may be necessary, but it is always a tragedy!

We might be able to prevent some divorces by tightening our divorce laws or by religious prohibitions against divorce, but such actions would not prevent broken marriages. When couples stay together only because of fear of the notoriety required by divorce laws, or because of church prohibitions, or *"for the sake of the children,"* tragedy can result. Disastrous marital triangles, domestic cruelty, child abuse, murder, and suicide are some of the documented consequences of marriage which had failed, but was not terminated. What a fearful choice! A broken home is a tragedy, but I will never forget a young man who put a gun barrel in his mouth and ended his marriage, his alternative to divorce. His church had forbidden divorce.

Our high divorce rate is not the real problem. Marriage failure comes first, and then divorce. The divorce rate is only an indicator of our high bad marriage rate. To correct this, we must do more than preach against divorce! It will be more difficult. It is easy to preach against divorce, but difficult for a church to be constructive in providing preparation for marriage and strengthening of marriages. Our challenge lies here!

Can a divorced person be ordained as a deacon or a preacher? The Apostle Paul, an educated man, knew the Greek word for *"divorce" (apostasion)* and knew his culture. He also knew Christ would accept anyone, even him, the *"chiefest of sinners"* (I Tim. 1:15). Unquestionably some early converts had multiple wives, slave wives, and concubines. Each of these relationships, though given the nicer title, polygamy, was adultery. Paul rejected the heads of such households as leaders in the church. The command to give a writing of divorcement in Deuteronomy 24 limited a man to only one wife and thus prohibited polygamy, and the adultery inherent in it. Paul seemed to concur fully when he said, "A bishop then must be blameless, the husband of one wife" (I Tim. 3:2). He rejected polygamy, not divorce.

Despite serious abuse, the divorce law (Deuteronomy 24) still has validity, Divorce is a radical solution to insurmountable marital problems. It ends all hope that the marriage might be saved, and declares publicly that the marriage has failed. This moment of truth can be shattering. Sin, related to this failure, must be confessed if there is to be any forgiveness, any peace with God, "If we confess our sin, he is faithful and just to forgive us our sin, and to cleanse us from all unrighteousness" (I John 1:9). This includes forgiveness for marital failure.

As opposed to putting away, written divorce, commanded by the law, provided a degree of human dignity for women subjected to cruel abuse, adulterous polygamy, and the whims of hard-hearted men. Nothing so flimsy as an oral "I divorce you" would do. Divorce declared the legal end of a marriage, thereby precluding any charge of adultery or bigamy should either party ever marry again. Divorce severed all marital ties and all control by the former spouse. Divorce demanded strict monogamy. Divorce prevented unilateral dismissal and preserved the basic right to be married. Divorce does the same today. Abandonment, desertion, putting away, or whatever one calls that hard-hearted forsaking of a wife for another, without divorce, was and is forbidden by the Lord Jesus himself (Mt. 19:9, Mt. 5:32, Mk. 10:11-12, Lk. 16:18).

For centuries much of the Christian community has interpreted these teachings of Jesus to say:

1) Divorce is absolutely not permitted, or at best, is permitted only in the case of admitted or proven adultery.
2) A divorced person is not allowed to marry again.
3) A divorced person who does marry again lives in adultery.
4) A person who is divorced cannot be ordained as a deacon or a minister.

Every one of these beliefs could be wrong. The first three are contrary to Mosaic Law and are based on scripture in which Jesus did not even use the Greek word for *"divorce" (apostasion);* the fourth is based on scripture in which Paul did not use it. The word Jesus used was *"apoluo,"* to put away. This was the problem with which he dealt, not divorce.

A divorced person must have great grace and determination to serve in a church which holds to the four positions listed above. How can this be, when the church is the body of Christ on earth, to function and to serve as he did, in person?

Christ, who once wept over Jerusalem must look down from heaven and weep over us. He came, and called Simon the Zealot, a radical anti-Roman, and Matthew, a hated lackey of Rome, a pair as incompatible as any you could find in America today; but he put them to work, together, in his kingdom. Then he went to Samaria, revealed himself to a woman with a shameful background of marital failures, and sent her out to share the revelation of God in Christ as if she were as good as anyone else. He must weep when he sees us wasting our time trying to figure out who we can disbar from serving him in his church.

Jesus openly ministered to all who came to him. Yet many of our divorced friends are afraid of our churches. They know what we say the Bible teaches about divorce. Can we be right and so unlike Christ? Do our traditional interpretations separate us from people whom Christ would have received? If so, we must be wrong. He came to save sinners. The only people he ever rejected were the self-righteously religious. Is our understanding of his words correct if it does not square with his life? Divorced people are real people! For centuries churches have excluded these people from fellowship and usefulness, from joy and equality, even from salvation, people for whom Christ died. Whether or not divorce is sin, this certainly is. May God grant us the grace to mediate that grace which did come in Jesus Christ to the divorced.

ONE

"FOR THE HARDNESS OF YOUR HEART"

I ALMOST REFUSED to perform their wedding. He was divorced and it was his fault. He admitted it. His fiancé was a Christian and he was not.

I had been a pastor for less than a year, but I knew we didn't believe in divorce. I also knew we didn't perform marriage ceremonies for divorced people, especially "guilty" parties such as he. But I had not yet been asked, as a pastor, to do so.

I couldn't say "no" when he called. I knew him. I liked him. Sure, he was a big, rough man who had a reputation, like his people. They all were rough, especially his father. I hadn't met his fiancée, who was from an adjoining state. She insisted he talk to a preacher and they have a Christian wedding, a church wedding.

I asked both of them to come talk to me. After they did, I still could not say "no." I told him what a difference my conversion had made after 18 years of marriage. His fiancée also shared her faith with him.

I had to think of the church also. I knew this could be a threat to the peace of our church. His reputation and our traditions were well known. Not only was he divorced and admittedly guilty of adultery, but I was also about to become involved in yoking together a Christian and a non-Christian, "unequals."

That was not bad enough, everyone must know. Church was her life. She wanted her people to come for the wedding, early on a Sunday morning in June; for me to invite all our church; for the wedding to be at 9:00 a.m., followed by coffee-cake and coffee; and for the whole wedding party to attend Sunday School and worship service together.

This is absolutely true, and this we would do. The fat was in the fire! Everyone would know what a heretic our little country church had for a pastor.

It was a beautiful wedding, not in the church, but under the large trees beside the church. The whole community came, and nearly all stayed for Sunday School and worship, including a large group of the bride's family and friends from the adjoining state.

That worship service was over-crowded and unforget-table. At the conclusion the big guy, the groom, committed his life to Christ, as did one of the bride's aunts, and another lady who was a friend of the bride, and another who was the wife of a friend of the groom.

And it didn't stop there. Within the next two years 14 of the groom's relatives, including his 68-year-old mother and 72-year-old father, became Christians.

> 3) And he answered and said unto them, What did Moses command you? 4) And they said, Moses suffered to write a bill of divorcement, and to put her away. 5) And Jesus answered and said unto them, For the hardness of your heart he wrote you this precept (Mark 10:3-5).

"For the hardness of your heart (Mark 10:5)." The big guy's heart had been hard; the record was undeniable. His first wife had suffered, and desperately needed him out of her life. She had been trapped in a broken marriage with a hard-hearted man. The divorce law freed her. A gift of God's love. But even hard-hearted people can change. He needed grace, too, and a gift of God's love, a new life. To help him find that, he needed a redemptive ministry, not a church that responded to his needs with equal hard-heartedness.

I felt what I had done was right. Yet I had no scriptural authority to do so. How could I be so right and so wrong? I was determined to find out. I knew God had to be more gracious than I was. I began, then and there, a most serious study that has gone on now for over 25 years.

I am convinced it was the Holy Spirit who would not allow me to say "no" when I knew it was the "thing to do," according to our tradition. I am also convinced it is the Holy Spirit who tells me we should carefully examine our traditions relating to divorce and remarriage in the church.

We, the church, and we as individuals do not have to protect people from God. But that is the way many attempt to handle the problems of divorce and remarriage. We step in and provide grace and love not available from God! EXAMPLES:

One church may tolerate divorce and remarriage of a member by determining that either or both were not Christians at the time of a previous marriage, and so were thus not "What God had joined together"; therefore were not under the prohibition: "Let not man put asunder." (Matthew 19:6). They are gracious and find a way around God's prohibition.

Another may make the judgment that the ones they choose to tolerate were not "the guilty parties," and thus grant them absolution and avoid the rigid strictures of scripture. What gracious judges they are.

Another grants annulments — as the Catholic Church recently did for Rep. Joseph Kennedy after 18 years of marriage, thus leaving his wife, mother of his 16-year-old twins, suddenly a woman who had never been married, and his sons illegitimate *(Kansas City Star,* April 29, 1997). Since God won't allow divorce and re-marriage, it is the only gracious thing to do. God won't help, so we will.

You see, we find a way to provide grace for people who need help, despite God's rules. We have forgotten that *God, not us, not even the church, is the source of grace and love.* We have become so totally bound by our theological doctrines and traditions that we absolutely refuse to seriously pray and search to find out what God is really like, as we have seen him in Christ; thus we fail to discover how he would

13

respond to people who need our help.

We have also developed a form of "biblical inerrancy" that amounts to no more than a conviction that we know the answers from familiar proof-texts and we have become inerrant to the degree that we often don't even attempt to look into the heart of God for our answers. We make our literal reading about ancient men's experiences with God our only guide for today. We thereby deny there is a Holy Spirit given to guide us in our daily struggles. Blasphemous!

To the church that tolerates second-marriage Christians because their first marriage was flawed by one or both being unbelievers, hog-wash! God used my marriage to provide my salvation. God loved me enough before I became a Christian to give me a wife and three fine sons who were born in wedlock. God's love (check out the New Testament if you don't believe this) is exactly the same for all people, good or bad, saints or sinners. "He sendeth rain on the just and unjust (Mt.5:45)."

To the church that makes the judgment that their friend is the "Innocent Party," I tell you on the basis of scripture you have no right to make that judgment, and probably more often than not are mistaken. In most divorces there is plenty of guilt for both parties.

To the Catholic Church, Sheila Rauch Kennedy, wife of Rep. Joseph Kennedy, in that April 29, 1997, *Kansas City Star* article, quoting from her recent book, Shattered Faith: A Woman's Struggle to Stop the Catholic Church from Annulling Her Marriage (Pantheon) writes this: "The annulment process is so hypocritical and so dishonest. It is important for children to know there are certain things you don't lie about because it is convenient." What audacity for the church to make itself a liar in order to protect its flock from a cruel God. What blasphemy! Is God the villain?

No! Divorce is a gift of God's love, and not only that, God permits valid re-marriage.

Divorces happen. Divorce is even commanded by Mosaic Law. That law provided for remarriage. Jesus, through whom grace and truth came, did not refute that law. For the law was given by Moses, but grace and truth came by Jesus Christ (John 1:17). Grace. We affirm Christ did bring grace, grace for our continuing lives beyond our salvation, brought to us by both his words and his life. In the study of divorce there may appear to be conflict between the examples set by Jesus and what we understand him to say.

From his life we see that he called people into his service regardless of their pasts — harlots, publicans, and a woman with five husbands to her record.

But what about his words? What about the words, "Whosoever putteth away his wife and marrieth another, committeth adultery," (Luke 16:18)? Does this sound like grace for the divorced? Are we sure we understand him?

From the life of Jesus we see an example of his grace when he accepted that woman at a well in Samaria as a person of real worth, and inspired her to tell her village (even the men) she had met the Christ. Some questions: (1) Was she really free from her past and a legitimate servant of God? (2) Does this compassion and forgiveness carry over to the divorced now? (3) Are people who are divorced and married to another really living in adultery, perpetually? (4) Is there no way to start again, free from their pasts? (5) Are they to be forever limited in their service to Christ?

Two verses from Luke make one concise comment on the matter:

> And it is easier for heaven and earth to pass, than one tittle of the law to fail. Whosoever putteth away his wife, and marrieth another, committeth adultery: and whosoever marrieth her that is put away from her husband committeth adultery (Luke 16:17-18).

Jesus made it clear that the Old Testament had something important to say. There is a specific law, and one that Jesus specifically refused to ignore or refute! He came to fulfill it.

When asked by the Pharisees, recorded in the Gospel of Mark, "Is it lawful for a man to put away his wife? (Mark

15

10:2)," Jesus answered, "What did Moses command you (Mark 10:3)?" "They said, Moses suffered to write a bill of divorcement ... (Mark 10:4)." There is an Old Testament Mosaic Law. In all my years of attending Sunday School I have never seen the following two verses included in the material studies.

Here is the law from Deuteronomy:

> When a man hath taken a wife, and married her, and it come to pass that she find no favour in his eyes, because he hath found some uncleanness in her: then let him write her a bill of divorcement, and give it in her hand, and send her out of his house. And when she is departed out of his house, she may go and be another man's wife (Deut. 24:1-2).

Many men ignored this law then and still do today, as we shall see later. But many married additional wives anyway. If a man did not divorce his wife, what did he do with her when he took another? He put her away, as stated in Luke 16:18. Put away. Not divorced. Really! There are two different Greek words. No! They are not synonyms, though virtually all men in Jesus' day considered them as such, they are not! One, "putting away," kept a woman enslaved, and was considered to be divorce by most men then; the other, "a writing of divorce," freed her to marry again.

Matthew 19:3-10 records the Pharisees taunting Jesus about this, asking him, "Is it lawful for a man to put away his wife for every cause?" He responded that marriage is a permanent relationship, for he said, "Whatsoever God hath joined together, let not man put asunder (Matt. 19:6)." This is what God has ordained. There is no conflict here. This I believe and practice! My wife and I have been married over 50 years.

They then asked, "Why did Moses then *command* to give a writing of divorcement, and to put her away (Matt. 19:7)?" (Both words are used here.) Jesus answered, "Because of the hardness of your hearts! (Matt. 19:8)." The God who is love had a reason to provide for divorce. God was always a God of love. Even before Christ came to make this so abundantly clear for those who had "eyes to see" and "ears to hear" there was a gift of God's love for those who had been thrown out of a marriage.

TWO

THE STRUGGLE FOR CONTROL

"FOR THE LAW WAS GIVEN by Moses, but grace and truth came by Jesus Christ (John 1:17)." So now, in the 20th century, nearly 2000 years after he came, how does grace come to those who have suffered the tragedy of a marriage failure and are divorced?

For centuries many churches have interpreted Jesus to teach: (1) Divorce is absolutely not permitted or, at best, is permitted only in the case of admitted or proven adultery; (2) A divorced person is not allowed to marry again; (3) A divorced person who does marry again lives in adultery; and (4) A person who is divorced cannot be ordained as a deacon, pastor, or other minister. If you were divorced, would that sound like grace?

I believe every one of these interpretations could be wrong. I don't mean to be presumptuous, but they could be the result of a misunderstanding of what Jesus said, based upon only one inconsistent translation of scripture, along with some deeply entrenched traditions, passed on to us from ancient cultures.

My conscience and my understanding of the Bible have been in tension for years over this matter. When Jesus seems to be hard-hearted, I believe I misunderstand him. As a pastor, I have observed that a divorced person must often exercise far greater grace than is extended by the church in order to find a place of service there. This is incredible, when we remember that the church is empowered to *be* the body of Christ on earth, to function and to serve as he did in person. Maybe the problem is with our grace, not with Christ's. Maybe others have been as careless as I have in really seeking to know how Christ would treat the divorced.

An astonishing variety of sinful people came to Jesus and through faith in him found themselves suddenly free and accepted, free to embark with him on a new life, free to serve God. That sounds like the work of grace. Their futures were no longer controlled only by their natural instincts, strengths and desires; their futures were no longer controlled even by religious tradition or Jewish laws; their futures were, instead, to be guided by the life and Spirit of the living Christ in a freedom never envisioned under the Law. *This* defines Christianity! Remember this!

Grace and truth had come to them in Jesus Christ. They were accepted, they were forgiven, they were free. "If therefore the son shall make you free, you shall be free indeed (John 8:36)." "But the preservation of freedom is an eternal struggle," Jefferson said. It was not long after the church was founded that Christians in Galatia were being harassed by Judaizers from Jerusalem, insisting they be circumcised before they could be "true" Christians. Freedom soon gave way to racial, social and gender discrimination in that congregation. The Apostle Paul's response to those who would legalistically impose these on those who were Christ's was quite clear:

> 23) But before faith came, we were kept under the law, shut up unto the faith which should afterwards be revealed. 24) Wherefore the law was our schoolmaster to bring us unto Christ, that we might be justified by faith. 25) But after that faith is come, we are no longer under a schoolmaster. 26) For ye are all the children of God by faith in Christ Jesus. 27) For as many of you as have been baptized into Christ have put on Christ. 28) There is neither Jew nor Greek, there is neither bond nor free, there is neither male nor female: for ye are all one in Christ Jesus. 29) And if ye be Christ's, then are ye Abraham's seed,

and heirs according to the promise (Gal. 3:23-29).

Man-made restrictions placed upon the status or service of any Christian are based upon an old covenant that is passing away, fulfilled by Christ through the cross and the resurrection.

> 10) For this is the covenant that I will make with the house of Israel after those days, saith the Lord; I will put my laws into their mind, and write them in their hearts: and I will be to them a God, and they shall be to me a people: 11) And they shall not teach every man his neighbour, and every man his brother, saying, Know the Lord: for all shall know me, from the least to the greatest. 12) For I will be merciful to their unrighteousness, and their sins and their iniquities will I remember no more. 13) In that he saith, A new covenant, he hath made the first old. Now that which decayeth and waxeth old is ready to vanish away (Heb. 8:10-13).

The old laws are not gone, but fulfilled, and when legalistically applied under the covenant of grace, become restrictions upon the free exercise of the work of the Holy Spirit, hindering the very life of the ever-present Christ in Christians. These actions are implications that the grace of Christ is not capable of personally guiding a person in what he or she may or may not do. To those who accept such restrictions, such interference in the work of Christ's forgiveness, Christ's calling, Christ's spirit in their lives, Paul gives a stern warning: "Christ is become of no effect unto you, whosoever of you are justified by the law; ye are fallen from grace (Gal. 5:4)." Serious, indeed!

If we accept Christ as "head over all things to the church, Which is his body ... (Eph. 1:22b-23a)," and if that body is to truly be "the fullness of him that filleth all in all (Eph. 1:23b)," then we must be careful not to hinder his Holy Spirit in the calling, the convicting, the saving and the employing of Christians in his service. The scripture records his calling to be personal to the one called, whether Jew or Gentile, slave or free, male or female, for all are the same in Christ (to paraphrase Gal. 3:28).

This thing about "neither male nor female" was new and radical — then. Christ upset things there — then. Women, too, can be called of God, can receive his spirit? But, one asks, "Doesn't the scripture say,

> 22) Wives, submit yourselves unto your own husbands, as unto the Lord. 23) For the husband is the head of the wife, even as Christ is the head of the church: and he is the saviour of the body. 24) Therefore as the church is subject unto Christ, so let the wives be to their own husbands in every thing (Eph. 5:22-24)?"

Is that the final word? Maybe not. There may be a balance to this, in Christ. You can get a clue that those verses may not be a license for autocratic male lordship when you read the next verse, "Husbands, love your wives, even as Christ also loved the church, and gave himself for it (Eph. 5:25)." God's way for men to behave toward their wives must also include Christ's example of servitude, his example of self-giving love, from husbands.

Traditional power and control are vital issues in the study of divorce and remarriage. The need arose for a "writing of divorce," a divorce decree, because it became necessary for God to deal with some men's improper, but traditionally accepted control of women. Jesus taught that God, even under the law, never intended for man to deal with his wife in such a way,

> 2) And the Pharisees came to him, and asked him, Is it lawful for a man to put away his wife? tempting him. 3) And he answered and said unto them, What did Moses command you? 4) And they said, Moses suffered to write a bill of divorcement, and to put her away. 5) And Jesus answered and said unto them, For the hardness

of your heart he wrote you this precept. 6) But from the beginning of the creation God made them male and female. 7) For this cause shall a man leave his father and mother, and cleave to his wife; 8) And they twain shall be one flesh. 9) What therefore God hath joined together, let not man put asunder (Mark 10:2-9).

Here we see what God expects of the marriage relationship. "One flesh," verse 8. That is not a lord and slave relationship! History shows us so many males dominated ancient cultures that we say, "Surely that is the way it is meant to be with a man and a woman." But is it the way of God or the way of man? We must look behind all our traditions and see what it was, in this imperfect world, which made divorce necessary in God's mind.

The command of God through Moses really existed. It is still there, in the 24th chapter of Deuteronomy. "Hardhearted men," Jesus said. The problem was that many of them married additional wives. I repeat, additional.

To God, this must have been a real shock. From the very beginning, he had seen that man needed the companionship of a mate, a woman: "And the Lord God said, It is not good that the man should be alone, I will make an help meet for him (Gen. 2:18)."

Then he established an almost unimaginable relationship for man and woman. He established an exclusive, permanent bonding that could only be described as "one flesh." Here is the record,

> 23) And Adam said, This is now bone of my bones, and flesh of my flesh: she shall be called Woman, because she was taken out of Man. 24) Therefore shall a man leave his father and his mother, and shall cleave unto his wife: and they shall be one flesh (Gen. 2:23-24).

This is marriage, God's first institution for the well-being of mankind. The special need we all have (both men and women) for such a mate is so great that divorce will become necessary, to declare that the right to be married has always been a basic human right, yes, even a basic necessity. Women need to be married, too.

But those ancient men, like men of today, could not be forced to love their wives or to be faithful; God has no puppets. And be aware that today this is not a problem brought about by men only. Yet God cared about those ancient women, their abuse, and their need to be married. Many had been deprived of that "one flesh" status, their true marital status, when their husbands destroyed that relationship by taking other wives, thus putting them out of that sacred one-flesh relationship. That is where the problem started. They needed help. God provided it.

Heartbreakingly real is the fact that marriage, God's first human institution, can be violated. Marriage, by God's grace, His first grant of a human right, is so sacred that it became necessary, upon violation, for God to command hard-hearted violators to acknowledge they had broken that sacred relationship, and to provide a writing of divorcement to women they put away, in order to restore grace to the women, the right to be married, even if she had been at fault. Ironic, isn't it, that marriage is so sacred that divorce became necessary?

The problem has ancient roots. Man's lust for more than he rightly ought to have began in the Garden of Eden, "Ye shall be as gods (Gen. 3:5)." Our ancestors spelled out our nature for us: "I want. I want all I can get. I want to be in control. God is not going to tell me what to eat and what not to eat." They said, "I'll take whatever I'm big enough to take, and I don't care what God or anyone else says, might makes right." Power. So whether it be the forbidden fruit in the Garden of Eden, another wife, a weaker race, a weaker business enterprise, or a weaker nation, man has traditionally said, "Might makes right, and I'll take what I can, do what I please."

How much of that ancient tradition of male domination of women was based upon the primordial supposition that "might makes right," and how much of it was really the will of God? I believe that in Christ we can see the answer to that question.

THREE

JUSTIFICATION BY TRADITION

THE LOVE OF POWER, of control, is one major factor in the hard-heartedness which led to the command to give a writing of divorce. Another factor affecting us now is justification by tradition. What I do is right, if it is the way the fathers did it.

We all have our traditions. Many are legitimate, proven, and of stabilizing value; but many of them may go untested for centuries as to their real worth. Not all religious traditions are bad; neither are all of them the will of God.

We are most comfortable following leaders who agree with our own traditional presuppositions. Good and sincere people can live under the gentle feeding of these traditions by committed leaders until they become group-approved and unquestioned doctrines believed to be basic to their faith. It had happened in the ancient Jerusalem to which Christ came. It can happen today in our churches.

During the life of Christ, certain leaders in Jerusalem were convinced that they were the caretakers of the world's only true religion. But they had problems. They considered the people of all other races to be inferior. They demanded strict adherence to their interpretations of the law as being the law itself. The poor and ill were neglected and oppressed, being judged as receiving from God the just rewards of their sins. By their traditions they justified severe oppression of women. Their interpretations of scripture allowed for slavery and unconscionable racial bigotry. Their methods of bringing people to their religion were totally counter-productive in mediating God's love. Claiming "the only true religion" as justification for their power, they built themselves a hollow dynasty, an inferior and actually illicit religion, totally devoid of the presence of God, but loyally and legalistically supported, often with self-sacrificial zeal.

The Jerusalem to which Jesus came therefore had a strong tradition of racial, gender, class, and religious discrimination.

To the leaders of this tradition—Jesus said:

13) But woe unto you, scribes and Pharisees, hypocrites! for ye shut up the kingdom of heaven against men: for ye neither go in yourselves, neither suffer ye them that are entering to go in. 14) Woe unto you, scribes and Pharisees, hypocrites! for ye devour widow's houses, and for a pretense make long prayer: therefore ye shall receive the greater damnation. 15) Woe unto you, scribes and Pharisees, hypocrites! for ye compass sea and land to make one proselyte, and when he is made, ye make him two-fold more the child of hell than yourselves (Matt. 23:13-15).

The scripture records: "He came unto his own, and his own received him not (John 1:11)." The Messiah came. He wasn't what they expected. He offered no land ... no earthly kingdom ... no power. And he could not tolerate their oppressive traditions. His coming created such an uproar that barely three years after he began his public ministry they killed him. Lest we ever think he would have us continue their traditions, he left these words:

34) 0 Jerusalem, Jerusalem, which killest the prophets, and stonest them that are sent unto thee; how often would I have gathered thy children together, as a hen doth gather her brood under her wings, and ye would not! 35) *Behold, your house is left unto you desolate:* and verily I say unto you, Ye shall not see me, until the time come when ye shall say, Blessed is he that cometh

in the name of the Lord (Luke 13:34-35). (Italics mine)

No wonder they killed him!

But have we learned anything from him? How may we profit from the Biblical record of his three short years of ministry?

The New Testament is our sacred record from those who knew him. It has proven itself a reliable guide to faith, but is in itself a reminder that it alone is not our only guide to life in faith; that we must also walk in the spirit. This is Christianity today. "He that hath not the spirit of Christ is none of his (Rom. 8:9)." "But the natural man receiveth not the things of the Spirit of God: for they are foolishness unto him: neither can he know them, because they are spiritually discerned (I Cor. 2:14)." We have a continuing need to really know the Bible. But along with that we need the guidance for our lives, which comes from the current life of the living Christ — his Spirit — to lead us in our understanding of the Bible,

> 13) Howbeit when he, the Spirit of truth, is come, he will guide you into all truth: for he shall not speak of himself; but whatsoever he shall hear, that shall he speak: and he will shew you things to come. 14) He shall glorify me: for he shall receive of mine, and shall shew it unto you (John 16:13-14).

We must reject any shackles anyone would forge from simplistic proof-texts of scripture as unquestionably the law of God. Though deeply entrenched, such may limit the freedom of Christ to guide us by his spirit. We must break the chains of guilt forced upon us by Christian traditions and be free to obey the Spirit of Christ.

Certainly tons and tons of references may be quoted to make a case for the traditional positions of the church pertaining to divorce and remarriage. These arguments are readily produced to defend our traditions as if no changes could be needed. Since publication of my article, "Divorce, the Law, and Jesus" by *Your Church* magazine in May/June 1986, I have received a number of letters from irate defenders of our traditions. But I have received over three times as many responses from people who share my concerns for ministry to the divorced, and who earnestly desire to do so without compromising scripture.

Requests for more information and for permission to reprint that article, coming from such diverse groups as Lutheran, Seventh Day Adventist, Church of God, Pentecostal, Episcopal, Church of Christ, Presbyterian, Methodist, Southern Baptist and American Baptist, may indicate that a wide spectrum of Christians are frustrated with our traditions. Anyone who knows many divorced people can attest to our failures in ministering to them. Indeed, one need not even look beyond the walls of the church to see the frustration and hurt.

Consider Harriet, who was divorced as a teen-ager, later became a Christian, and is now middle-aged and married to Herman. Harriet is guilt-ridden because at church she was told she is "living in adultery." Her pastor constantly assures her the church loves her; yet he preaches that one married after divorce lives in adultery. She feels her church condemns her, but condescends to love her anyway. Her pastor's own testimony, which I heard him give in a sermon, was that when she approached him to discuss the subject, he said to her, "Either you believe the Bible or you don't," and dismissed her. He was thereby convincing us that he was a "true Bible believer." Is it actually the will of God for her to have no peace and no place of service at church in her present married life? Yet, can we gloss over scripture and imply that God, as a loving and forgiving God, forgives her for living in adultery, even though, according to her understanding of scripture, she continues to do so?

There is a conflict here, if marriage after divorce really is living in adultery. Something is wrong if we must merely overlook adultery and condescend to her and treat her nicely anyway. Does her second marriage constitute adultery? If so, what must she do to please God and the church? Must she get rid of Herman and spend the rest of her years alone? Neither way makes sense, and we know it.

The words of Christ are, "Come unto me, all ye that labor and are heavy laden, and I will give you rest (Matt. 11:28)." I have made personal efforts to minister to the divorced and include them in the ministry of the church, and have seen our own people use some scriptural proof text in such a way as to make it God's word of rejection for them. They are undoubtedly sincere, but this likely comes second-handed, as a defense of tradition that appears to be cultural, ingrained, a rote response which has been handed down. It is time to stop and think!

Let me tell you a true story. Three other local pastors and I were on a trip to Louisiana to a conference, and a discussion of the "second coming" developed, in fact, a heated discussion. During a lull, one of the pastors was asked, "What did Jesus say about that?" He immediately responded, "I don't care what Jesus said, I know what I believe." He never realized he said that. If he had thought, I'm sure he would not have said it. But that was his "off the top of his head" response. Do we really care what Jesus really said? It's time to stop and think.

We do not have any record in the Bible of Christianity being practiced in a Christian culture. It wasn't here yet, and still isn't! All of the New Testament writers record the activities of early Christians in places dominated by strong pagan or Jewish traditions. We all have to live and operate within some traditions in order to receive any acceptance at all. Remember that the apostle Paul, who preached so vehemently against Judaizers in Galatia who would have Christians first be circumcised, is the same Paul who earlier took the young Timothy and circumcised him because his father was a Greek, and "because of the Jews which were in those parts (Acts 16:3)." We cannot merely ignore our culture. They were no different then.

Many churches do not ordain divorced men as deacons or ministers now. Their local cultures have never allowed that. We live and work within certain real conditions with which we may or may not agree, but within which we must work, if we work at all. I am certain that some of the constraints voiced by Paul in Corinth were for the same reason.

Paul could not have worked effectively within the turmoil he would have created had he sent a woman to preach in a Jewish synagogue, nor had he even allowed one to stand and question a male speaker in public. It wasn't done in that society. What he did then was necessary, but *may not be necessary today.* God does not expect us to treat one another as some hard-hearted men treated women in Old Testament days. Traditions are not binding on us as Christians; the will of God is. Really! Grace and truth did come by Jesus Christ. He did not refute the grace given through Moses in the law. Christ did not take away God's grace. He brought more!

FOUR

THE CRUX OF THE MATTER:
"I HATE PUTTING AWAY," SAITH JEHOVAH

MANY OF US would remove the barriers between our churches and the divorced. But in order to do so honestly, we must not compromise the teachings of scripture. We must not only rejoice in the grace that came in Christ, but also find the truth of the mind of Christ for our needs now. We must interpret scripture in a totally honest manner, examining our traditions in the light of Christ, sparing ourselves none of the pain that may come with change. "For the law was given by Moses, but grace and truth came by Jesus Christ (John 1:17)."

There is a danger that we will close our eyes to conflicting evidence if we are deeply committed to a hope or a belief, or are emotionally supportive of people we see as mistreated or suffering.

William Barclay, probably the best known British expositor of the Bible, in a little paperback, *Introducing the Bible* (Abingdon Press, 1972), says:

> The student of the Bible must study the Bible honestly. This is to say, he must go to the Bible to find and to seek the truth, and not to prove a case about which he has already made up his mind. It is common — it is almost usual — for people to use the Bible as an arsenal of proof texts to prove things about which they have already made up their minds. A man can use the Bible to find in it what he wants to find. He can use it

to hear the echo of his own voice rather than the sound of the voice of God. Tyndale once said that the students who were taught by the priests and the monks came to the Bible "armed with false principles, with which they are clean shut out of the understanding of Scripture." Arminius once said: "Nothing is more obstructive to the investigation of the truth than prior commitments to partial truths." This is simply to say that not even God can teach a man who comes to the Bible with his mind made up (p. 93).

With that in mind, now, for the crux of the matter. I see some distinctions between some key words in the Old Testament and between some words Christ spoke in the Gospels, distinctions never pointed out to me. Those different words, "put away" and "writing of divorcement" are different in Greek, the language of the New Testament of Christ's time and the Old Testament. They are different! If my solution is not valid, that does not prove there is no problem, nor does it give us permission to sweep the matter back under the carpet and go on failing people for whom Christ died.

Edward B. Lindaman, a space-age scientist, said it well quoting a poem written by Ward Kaiser:

This is not the future's first burst.
Always it keeps coming, at supersonic speed.
Suddenly in the desert stands John the Baptist
"Repent," he shouts, "the future, God's future, is at hand.
It will not wait!"
And so Jesus comes.
Are we ready? Do we welcome him?
Do we love Him, do we serve Him
Do we see Him for who He is?
Or, do we go on hating the Romans,
Talking about the price of eggs.
Still the future speeds,
Tomorrow starts today.

People move, cities grow,
Things change.
In the name of God we must do better than before
The future will not wait.

(Ward Kaiser; *What Will Life Be Like in the 1970's?* Edward B. Lindaman, printed in *Review and Expositor,* Vol. LXVII, No. 1, Winter 1970.)

Most people in the United States are closely related to at least one divorced person, but many cannot even talk about Christ or the church with that person. Yet, as a Baptist, I must admit that the percentage of people in our cities who are Baptists is considerably less than it was in 1900, including such strongholds where Baptist empires abound as Atlanta and Dallas. Our failure to examine our traditions may well be one reason for our failure in these and other cities.

The Gospel of John teaches us that Jesus is the ultimate revelation of God:

> 1) In the beginning was the Word, and the Word was with God, and the Word was God. 2) The same was in the beginning with God. 3) All things were made by him; and without him was not any thing made that was made. 4) In him was life; and the life was the light of men (John 1:1-4).

Believing this, we must take care not to determine God's will for his church today by entrenched power or Old Testament traditions. We must learn the mind of God, from the words, the life, and the Spirit of Christ — no less than all three! We must study his words until we come to an understanding of them that the Holy Spirit assures us squares with his life. Now, "The future will not wait."

As a child in Sunday School I developed the notion that "God's People" did no wrong, that everybody on God's side did right. We were given some kind of justification for every unthinkable thing some of them did. This is pure childish fantasy. God put up with and used people who were far from perfect.

According to God's standards for monogamous marriage, only one of Solomon's 700 wives could have been that "one flesh," could have been "What God hath joined together." Solomon also had 300 concubines.

If he did not divorce her, what did a man of those days do with a wife who "Finds no favour in his eyes?" He put her away. There is a word for it in the Old Testament, the Hebrew word *shalach*. God did this to Israel, recorded in Jeremiah 3. It is different than the Hebrew word for divorce, which is *keriythuwth*. *Keriythuwth* (Jer. 3:8), literally meaning excision, a cutting of the marital bond, legal divorce; was to be written, as commanded in Deuteronomy 24, and permitted subsequent marriage for the wife. God did this to Israel, also.

This practice of putting away, *shalach,* when the woman was orally dismissed, was their "semi-divorce." (One-half of the marriage dismissed!) and was sometimes called divorce. A tradition developed whereby a man merely said, "I divorce thee," and that "divorce" was not contestable, but was not a legal divorce for the woman. *This word described a cruel tradition, which made Deuteronomy 24 a necessity.* But even that law providing for divorce, which met a need then, in that male-dominated society before Christ came, was often ignored, and is being ignored even today.

It happened in the time of Moses; it happened in the time of Christ and Josephus; and, believe it or not, it happens *today!* I quote from the *Wichita Beacon* (Wichita, Kansas) of February 20, 1988:

DIVORCE CHANGE REQUESTED

NEW YORK— In a study of religiously observant Jewish women in broken marriages, Benita Gayle-Almeleh of the American Jewish Committee, has urged rabbinical action to remedy the paradoxical plight of thousands of Jewish women unable to obtain a religious divorce.

"She's in a limbo, neither married, nor unmarried," said Gayle-Almeleh of Jewish women divorced by civil action, but whose civilly divorced husbands won't grant a religious bill of divorcement called a *get.*

According to Jewish law as observed in Conservative and Orthodox Judaism, only the man can grant a get.

If he refuses, the woman's marriage, though ended civilly, is still binding religiously.

In such circumstances, said Gayle-Almeleh, a woman is "not free to remarry, to pick up the pieces and go on with her life."

Gayle-Almeleh estimates at least 35,000 Jewish women across the country are trapped in that situation.

Here, even in America, these men "put away" their wives through misuse of civil law, but retain power over them by ignoring the religious law given to provide the women freedom when put away by hard-hearted husbands. "When a *man* ..." the letter of the Mosaic Law commanded.

Patriarchs such as Solomon did not always abandon their wives when they married others. They also practiced polygamy, a modified form of putting away. In its favor, polygamy did not leave a wife cut off and destitute, as apparently happened in many cases of putting away, but it deprived her of the status of wife, wherein the "two became one." No true "forsaking of all others" can possibly exist in polygamy.

Some of the hardships and terror experienced by women who were "put away" can be seen as this Hebrew word *shalach* is described in the helpful little *Langenscheid Pocket Hebrew Dictionary* (McGraw-Hill, 1969)— "to let loose, roaming at large, to be scared, abandoned, forsaken (p. 352)." J. B. Phillips, in his book of meditations *For This Day* (Word, 1975) wrote:

> The Christian faith took root and flourished in an atmosphere almost entirely pagan, where cruelty and sexual immorality were taken for

granted, where slavery and the inferiority of women were almost universal, while superstition and rival religions with all kinds of bogus claims, existed on every hand.

God hated this "putting away." Malachi, the last Old Testament prophet, broken-heatedly pleaded with God's people to stop the practice. Hear Malachi plead with them. The word translated "putting away" in Mal. 2:16 is *not keriythuwth,* the Hebrew word for divorce, but it is *shalach,* put away. Hear Malachi respond to leaders who asked how they had dealt treacherously, and had committed abomination in Israel, and had profaned the holiness of the Lord.

14) Yet ye say, Wherefore? Because the Lord hath been witness between thee and the wife of thy youth, against whom thou hast dealt treacherously: yet is she thy companion, and the wife of thy covenant. 15) And did not he make one? Yet had he the residue of the spirit. And wherefore one? That he might seek a godly seed. Therefore take heed to your spirit, and let none deal treacherously against the wife of his youth. 16) For the Lord, the God of Israel, saith that he hateth *putting away:* for one covereth violence with his garment, saith the Lord of hosts: therefore take heed to your spirit, that ye deal not treacherously (italics mine) (Mal. 2:14-16).

This practice was cruel and was adulterous, *but it was not true divorce, full divorce, for both man and woman.* This was much worse, ignoring the wife's welfare.

Malachi said, of the "wife of thy youth," "yet is she thy companion." Apparently she was still around, and not to be ignored. Obviously she had not married another, "Yet is she thy companion, and the wife of thy covenant." If she had been divorced and then married, the law would have forbidden the husband of her youth to take her back, and Malachi would not have demanded it. She could not marry another because she was still married. Men were "treacherously" dealing with their wives in putting them away. Josephus, Esdras (both apocryphal and the biblical Ezra), and Nehemiah indicate that many of the men were taking younger wives from other races.

The *Antiquities of the Jews,* from *The Life and Works of Josephus,* Whiston, reveals how common it was at the time Christ lived for men to take wives and leave them at will.

A man named Joseph, Ptolemy's representative and tax collector in Jerusalem, a Jew, illustrates the frustration experienced by Malachi: "This good fortune he enjoyed for twenty-two years, and was become the father of seven sons by one wife; he had also another son, whose name was Hyrcanus, by his brother Solymius' daughter, whom he married on the following occasion (12.4.6.p. 358)."

The "occasion" referred to is a long story of intrigue and duplicity, but the gist of it is: Joseph totally disregarded the wife of his youth and the mother of his seven sons and married and had a child by another (his niece). His first wife was simply "put away." How? Who knows? She was a woman, and in that era, in that tradition, her status was not worthy of mention.

Malachi didn't like it! I don't think Jesus liked it either. Many of us have heard numerous sermons on "God Hates Divorce" based on this passage in Malachi about "putting away." The prophet Malachi was a devout observer of the Mosaic Law. It had been around a long time. Being such, he could never àsk a man to take back a woman who had been given a writing of divorcement, legally divorced, so that hadn't happened to the true wives.

That writing of divorce would have permitted a wife to marry another man, legally; that writing would have severed all connection with her former husband, and that writing would have forbade her re-marrying her former husband if she had married another.

It appears that men did what men of that era commonly did, despite the law. They put away, "dealt treacherously with," their wives, ignoring *their* right to be married. Call it what you will, abandoned, in some cases; set aside but kept (polygamy), in others; but, in any case, men married whom they would. Jesus would call it adultery. Malachi understood God didn't like it. Malachi told the men to quit betraying their true wives, the one true wife, the first wife, the wife of the covenant, the wife of their youth. Quit committing adultery. Forsake polygamy. But he didn't mention divorce.

Maybe the women would have fared as badly "divorced" as they did "put away," in that age, maybe not. Moses had some reason to command it. At least the distinction must be made. We will soon discover two Greek words with the same distinction in the New Testament.

We have, in Leviticus 21:14, 22:13, and Numbers 30:9, some isolated references to divorced women. The word translated divorce in all these cases is another word, the Hebrew word *garash,* meaning "to drive out from a possession," and was divorce only in the sense that the women had been driven out. The word used is the very same word repeatedly used in Exodus (6:1; 23:28, 29,30, 31; 33.2; 34:11) when the Bible spoke of driving out the Canaanites and Hivites from the land. It also, like *shalach,* is a harsh word, "to thrust out," containing none of the protection for women of Deut. 24:1-3, and the word for written divorce, *keriythuwth,* in her hand.

I point this out to say that men in Old Testament days, even Jewish men, did not all subscribe to the "one flesh" concept of Genesis, or the "husband of one wife" concept to be spelled out later by Paul in the New Testament. And they were stunned at the "Till death do us part" concept so forcefully given them by Christ, recorded in Matthew 19. In most cases they took a woman into the tent, were observed to do so, and were considered married. They could toss a woman out, or push her aside, and might say, orally, "I divorce you," and that was that! But that did not satisfy the law Moses wrote, "Give her a writing of divorcement."

The law could not make a man love his wife. Laws do not change human nature. The law could make him give her a writing of divorcement and renew her sacred right to be married if he abandoned her, theoretically.

In Judaism, as in many other religions, some even labeled "Christian," men are traditionally authorized to "divorce" their wives, to take additional wives while previous wives are not given a proper and releasing writing of divorcement. *They* call it "divorce," their oral divorce or their polygamy, when they know it is not. *They* may be divorced, but their wives are not.

This practice was not divorce in Jesus' day, and it is not divorce today. Scholars today say you can make no distinction between the two words "because they were used synonymously (letter received from Judson Press, Dated December 19, 1997)." *Yes, they were,* and are, by *hardhearted men. That* is what Deuteronomy 24:1-2 was all about. That is what Matthew 19:7-8 was about. They are not *synonymous* words. They are really *antonymous!* They are the difference between slavery and freedom for one-half of humanity, women.

FIVE

AND JESUS CAME

JESUS CAME. And his words do not deny his actions! He spoke of this cruel practice when he said, "Whosoever putteth away his wife, and marrieth another, committeth adultery (Luke 16:18)!" We could have misunderstood him. We could have heard him say, "Whosoever divorces his wife," when he actually did say, "Whosoever puts away his wife."

This New Testament word, translated "put away" in the King James Version, is a form of the Greek word *apoluo*. It is the word in Greek which parallels that Old Testament Hebrew word *shalach* (put away). It is the word Jesus used here, in Luke 16:18.

There are two biblical words that technically mean divorce, the Old Testament Hebrew word *keriythuwth,* and the New Testament Greek word, *apostasion. The Arndt-Gingrich Lexicon of the New Testament* cites usage of the word *apostasion* as the technical term for a bill or writing of divorce as far back as 258 B.C.

This word denotes true, wife-releasing divorce and was not used here in Luke 16:18. Many use the two Greek words of the New Testament, *apoluo* and *apostasion* as synonyms. I believe they were, to hard-hearted men who had no concept that women should have any rights. I believe, in the mind of Jesus, who cared about women, there was a distinct difference. To *unilaterally* divorce one's self from a person or position is not at all equivalent to granting to a woman a written divorce. *Apoluo* is always unilateral. There are distinctions between the two words. A woman could not marry

41

again after this traditional oral "divorce."

A form of the verb *apoluo,* used here, describes what many men traditionally did in those days, unilaterally. Marriage should be permanent. But rampant, "for any cause" dismissal, putting away - men divorcing themselves *without giving a divorce* — was obscene. Divorce *is* better than that. God, permitting us freedom, does not abrogate the free will of a person. A person can be cruel, but God never fails to care about the victims of our free will. It goes like this: God cares first; then through inspiration from him, we care.

It seems evident that Jewish home life, under the Law, was of a higher moral character than some in that male-dominated world. Even so, the evidence indicates little if any social stigma against the practices of multiple wives, slave wives, and concubines. Also, as we look at the teachings of Jesus, we must remember that many of his audience were not Jewish.

Maybe large numbers of common men didn't customarily put aside their wives or take additional wives without giving written divorce, but we have plenty of evidence of disregard for the rights of women and proof that some did, indicating the likelihood that this was the problem Jesus was addressing when he said, "Whosoever putteth away his wife . . . (Luke 16:18)."

We do know that women were often ignored, even in such Gospel accounts as the feeding of the multitudes by Christ. In the record of the people who returned to Jerusalem from Babylon, pages of men are listed; musicians and singers are numbered; even the camels, horses, mules and asses are there in the record. Wives and daughters are not mentioned.

We know that polygamy had become commonplace, especially among the wealthy.

We know that in that region oral divorce still remains, and is still the privilege of men only.

Both polygamy and oral divorce come under the meaning of the word *apoluo,* failure to observe the nicety of a writing of divorcement, resulting for many in the practice of polygamy. Meeting these abominations head-on did not contradict Christ's affirmation of the Deuteronomic law; rather, his actions underscored the need for the law.

The Jewish law demanding written divorce (Deut. 24:1-2) could be ignored without social stigma or legal recourse, and, as seen in the "Beacon," can still be ignored. If a man married another woman, so what? If a man "put away" *(apoluo)"* his wife without bothering with a divorce ("get") who was going to object? The woman? In that land, as opposed to the current problem of the 35,000 Jewish women needing a religious divorce in America, religious law was also the civil law. Those women had no rights, civil or religious.

Jesus had some objections. Jesus loved even mistreated women! He told them that this earth would go up in smoke before the law against putting away without a written bill of divorce should fail. In this context he said:

> 17) And it is easier for heaven and earth to pass, than one tittle of the law to fail. 18) Whosoever putteth away his wife, and marrieth another, committeth adultery: and whosoever marrieth her that is put away from her husband committeth adultery (Luke 16:17-18).

Therefore, when you put away a wife (without written divorce), and marry another (while still married), you are guilty of adultery (Lk. 16:18). Moreover, she has no divorce, but is an abandoned *married* woman. Any man marrying her would commit adultery (Lk. 16:18), the same moral problem 35,000 Jewish women who have been put away by means of civil decree, but still married according to Jewish religious law (Deut. 24), face in modern America.

The distinction between "put away" and "divorce" between the Greek *apoluo* and *apostasion* is critical. *Apoluo* dismissed the woman, but left her married, put away, with no rights, no recourse, and deprived of the basic right to monogamous marriage. *Apostasion* ended marriage and permitted a legal subsequent marriage. The paper makes a difference. "Let him write a bill of divorcement, and give it in her hand, and send her out of his house. And when she is departed out of his house, she may go and be another man's wife (Deut. 24:2)." That is the law of Moses.

Now for those other passages, other than Lk. 16:17-18 where Jesus spoke of this matter and your Bible may use the word "divorce." They include Matt. 19:9, Mark 10:10-12, and Matt. 5:32. Mark 10:12 makes it clear that Jesus did not exempt women from rules of behavior he gave the men: "And if a woman shall put away her husband, and be married to another, she committeth adultery." This was new! Jewish women had never heard of any such possibility.

Jesus used a form of the word *apoluo* eleven times in these passages pertaining to divorce and remarriage. In every passage he forbade *apoluo,* putting away. He *never* forbade giving *apostasion,* written divorce, as required by Jewish law.

This study will focus on Matthew chapter 5, verses 31 and 32, as they appear in the King James Version of the Bible, because I believe the problem began there:

> 31) It hath been said, Whosoever shall put away his wife, let him give her a writing of divorcement: 32) but I say unto you, That whosoever shall put away his wife, saving for the cause of fornication, causeth her to commit adultery: and whosoever shall marry her that is divorced committeth adultery (Matt. 5:31-32).

Here, in the last line, the word translated "divorced" is an *inconsistency in translation* where I believe much of the trouble began. There! That word is translated "divorced."

That one Greek word which made the difference is *apoluo* and words derived from it. Forms of that word are translated "put away" in ten places pertaining only to marital separation in the King James Version of the Bible; *every place* a form of it appears — *except this one place.* In this one eleventh place, near the end of this verse, it was translated "divorced," in 1611. "And whosoever shall marry her that is *divorced* committeth adultery *(italics mine)."*

In the *entire* New Testament, forms of *apoluo* appear a total of 69 times, but *only in this one instance* is it translated "divorced." If that word had been translated in harmony with the rest of the King James Version, it would say, "And whosoever shall marry her who has been put away (or abandoned, or dismissed, etc.) committeth adultery."

Maybe Jesus *really* was *not talking about divorce.* Those modern Jewish women reported on in "The Beacon" are not divorced according to their religious law. They are put away. The first part of Matt. 5:32 literally says "whosoever shall put away his wife." Same word! It does not say "divorce." *Apostasion* is the Greek word for written divorce. Since Jesus did not *speak* of giving a divorce here, he surely did not *mean* divorce and it could make a world of difference. He was speaking of something else men did: marry another *without* a divorce, "put away," a wife, still married, *not* divorced at all, just like those 35,000 Jewish women in America, waiting for their men to decide to obey the Jewish law. Abomination!

Now look at this: the *Holy Bible From the Ancient Eastern Text,* Matt. 5:32b reads, "And whosoever marries a woman who is separated, but not divorced, commits adultery." In this text Luke 16:18b reads, "He who marries the one who is illegally separated commits adultery." This translation highlights the misunderstanding made possible by that inconsistent King James translation of Matt. 5:32. *(Holy Bible from the Ancient Eastern Text: George M. Lamsa's Translation from the Aramaic of the Peshitta.)* (Harper & Row, Publishers, San Francisco, pp 955, 1038).

If a man and woman are joined under God in a true marriage relationship, that man and that woman attain a supreme state of equality. The two become one. "So ought men to love their wives as their own bodies. He that loveth his wife loveth himself (Eph. 5:28)." This leaves no room for control or cruelty. Even if tradition allows it, love does not! To be deprived of marriage or to have another woman added to a marriage was to relegate the wife to the role of an inferior, to love her less than self, to say the least. The kind of God who is and always has been love, the one we know in Christ, has surely always cared about such mistreated people. That is why we care.

Though we can't go back and see first-hand what Jesus intended to correct in that culture, we do know that from the very beginning Christianity has insisted upon the practice of monogamous marriage.

Isn't it obvious there was some "no-man's-land" then in that society wherein women, like the 35,000 Jewish women in America now, were neither married nor divorced? Wasn't there some dreadful status wherein women were left stranded, "put away," dismissed, no longer married, but not totally divorced from their marriages? Yes! Clearly!

When Jesus quoted, "It hath been said, Whosoever shall put away his wife, let him give her a writing of divorcement (Matt. 5:31)," he quoted Deut. 24:1-2 where we see the basic purpose for divorce. It continues, "... And give it in her hand and send her out of his house. And when she is departed out of his house, she may go and be another man's wife (Deut. 24:1-2)."

SIX

WHY WASN'T IT CORRECTED?

WHY WASN'T THAT less than precise 1611 translation of *apoluo* in Matthew 5:32 corrected? The truth is, it was! And the correction was ignored. Why? Tradition probably prevailed.

It was corrected, but few noticed! *Where? How?* In the very literal American Standard Version (ASV) *apoluo* is always translated "put away." The other word, *apostasion,* is always translated "divorce" or "a writing of divorce."

This correction appeared in the American Standard Version of 1901, following the English Revision in 1881-1885 of their own 1611 King James Version. But 270 years of tradition had its effect. A man recently said, "If you do something three Sundays in a row in a Baptist Church, you have established a tradition." Imagine overcoming 270 years of reading "divorced." That 1611 King James Version mistranslation in this one instance has so dominated our thinking that virtually all modern translations say "divorced," not just in that one place, but in *all eleven places.* They completely ignore the correction provided by the 1901 American Standard Version, and ignore the distinction between the two words.

Two English words we use to describe marital break-up are separation and divorce. Our word "separation" may or may not include divorce. "Divorced" declares that a marriage is over, *legally* ended. The difference is significant. The Greek word *apoluo* meant dismissal by the husband and may not have included a writing of divorce. *Apostasion* was specific, it did; it was the technical term for the writing of divorcement. It had that primary meaning at the time of the writing of the New Testament. *The Arndt-Gingrich Greek-Lexicon of the New Testament* (University of Chicago Press, 1957) states of *apostasion:*

> A legal t.t. [technical term] found as early as 258 B.C ... [numerous early usages are cited] in the sense of relinquishment of property after sale, abandonment, etc. The consequent giving up on one's own claim explains the meaning which the word acquires in Jewish circles: (Jer. 3:8) give (one's wife) a certificate of divorce (Matt. 19:7) (p. 97).

It is interesting to note when reading the King James Version that tradition has conditioned us to think "divorced" in all those eleven places in which forms of *apoluo* appear, even though our eyes literally read "put away" ten times out of the eleven. Why is this so? Why was it not corrected? I repeat: it was, and the correction was ignored!

With "divorced" in our minds instead of "separated, but not divorced" or "put away" we have assumed that anyone who *divorces* his wife and marries another commits adultery. We have assumed "divorced" was said in these passages when in every instance the Greek text actually says "put away." Would our theology be different today if that word had been consistently translated "put away?"

The King James Version of the Bible (KJV) was translated in 1611 in England by order of the king. It was put into beautiful language, "Appointed to be read in churches" (from the cover page). For many people, it alone is "The Bible."

No book has ever meant as much to as many people as the King James Version of the Bible has. Therefore, we are responsible to see that a translator's slip such as was made in Matt. 5:32 is made known, especially when the people responsible for the translation have openly published a corrected version.

New translations do not deliver us from the responsibility for correcting and interpreting this one properly. Not only is it still widely used, but modern translators are strongly influenced by it. It came on the scene early in the history of printed matter, shortly after the advent of the printing press. It has lived along side of, and has thereby influenced, nearly everything ever to come off any British or American printing press, and probably is the best-known printed matter on earth. A lot of Christians find it difficult to believe that there could be a mistranslation of any kind in the King James Version of the Bible.

The scholar who translates scripture today cannot even get beyond the influence of the King James Version. He probably grew up memorizing it. All our English lexicons have been written under the influence of it, and may list "divorced" as a meaning of *apoluo,* based upon the King James tradition. It permeates our society, and justly so. Interpretations and word usage inherited from it are a part of our lives and the make-up of those who now translate and interpret scripture.

The Greek word for divorce is *apostasion.* In the King James Version the word *apoluo,* which did not necessarily include divorce, was translated "divorce" in one place. Modern translations almost invariably translate that word "divorce," *despite the English correction in 1881-1885, and the American Standard Version correction in 1901.* These seem to be *intentional corrections* and were published to make them known. They were not used in translating the generally excellent Revised Standard Version of 1946 and 1952, and also by most other modern translations since then, most of which are otherwise superb.

A serious question about translations arises here. Deut. 24:1-4 is translated in the King James and the old *corrected* American Standard Version of 1901 *as a commandment* to a man who finds fault with his wife to write her a bill of divorcement and send her out of his house, so that she may go and be another man's wife. If she marries another, he is instructed never to take her back. Note the tone of authority in this American Standard Version of 1901.

1) When a man taketh a wife, and marrieth her, then it shall be, if she find no favor in his eyes, because he hath found some unseemly thing in her, that he shall write her a bill of divorcement, and give it in her hand, and send her out of his house. 2) And when she is departed out of his house, she may go and be another man's wife. 3) And if the latter husband hate her, and write her a bill of divorcement, and give it in her hand, and send her out of his house; or if the latter husband dies, who took her to be his wife; 4) her former husband, who sent her away, may not take her again to be his wife, after that she is defiled; for that is abomination before Jehovah: and thou shalt not cause the land to sin, which Jehovah thy God giveth thee for an inheritance (Deut. 24:1-4, ASV).

That is the *corrected* version of 1901. But, the Revised Standard Version (1952), ignoring the difference between *apoluo* and *apostasion*, is translated so that it does not command a man to give his wife a divorce if she finds no favor in his eyes, but states that if he does give her a writing of divorce, and if he sends her out, and if she marries another, then he may not take her back. Note the conditional tone in it.

1) When a man takes a wife and marries her, if then she find no favor in his eyes because he has found some indecency in her, and he writes her a bill of divorce and puts it in her hand and sends her out of his house, and she departs out of his house, 2) and if she goes and becomes another man's wife, 3) and the latter husband dislikes her and writes her a bill of divorce and puts it in her hand and sends her out of his house, or if the latter husband dies, who took her to be his wife, 4) then her former husband, who sent her away, may not take her again to be his wife, af-

ter she has been defiled; for that is an abomination before the Lord, and you shall not bring guilt upon the land which the Lord your God give you for an inheritance (Deut. 24:1-4, RSV.).

Our tradition, because the mistranslation of *apoluo* in the popular King James Version forbids marrying again after divorce, and this tradition presses for that doctrine to be included in the translation of the Revised Standard Version of 1952, which, in all 11 instances mistranslates *apoluo.* Consider this: (1) If the Revised Standard Version is correct, there is no *command* to give a writing of divorce in the Old Testament, and Deut. 24 is *only* a commentary on divorce decree which nowhere else appears, so there is thus no legitimate divorce decree in the Bible which could be understood by the people when Jeremiah said that God sent Israel away because of her adulteries *and* gave her a writing of divorcement (Jer. 3:8); (2) In Mark 10:3 (All translations) Jesus is recorded as saying "What did Moses *command?*" when referring to Deut. 24. The word is *eneteilato,* demanding only that translation; (3) In Matt. 19:7, (All translations) "They say unto him, Why did Moses then *command (eneteilato)* to give a writing of divorcement, and to put her away?" (again referring to Deut. 24); (4) Deut. 24 is a part of the Jewish books of the law, "The Torah" and Flavius Josephus, the historian who lived in the time of Christ stated:

He that desires to be divorced from his wife for any cause whatsoever, (and many such causes happen among men), let him in writing give assurance that he will never use her as his wife any more; for by this means she may be at liberty to marry another husband, although before this bill of divorce be given, she is not to be permitted so to do . . . (Antiquities of the Jews (The Life and Work of Flavius Josephus), IV. 8. 23 p. 134; (tr. Wm. Whiston; Holt, Rinehart, and Winston, N.Y.).

Notice the words "let him in writing give assurance." The bill of divorce was the enabling instrument, and it alone fulfilled God's requirement for granting freedom to the evicted wife.

That this relates to Deuteronomic Law is affirmed by the fact that not only this passage but virtually all 49 sections of Book IV, Chapter VIII of Josephus are paraphrases of Deuteronomic Law and are entitled "The Polity Settled by Moses; and How He Disappeared from Mankind." Throughout his work Josephus refers to them as, "The law of the Jews." In XV. 7. 10, p. 462 Josephus also states:

> But some time afterward, when Salome happened to quarrel with Costobarus, she sent him a bill of divorce, and dissolved her marriage with him, though this was not according to the Jewish laws; for with us it is lawful for a husband to do so; but a wife, if she departs from her husband, cannot of herself be married to another, unless her former husband put her away. However, Salome chose to follow not the law of her country, but the law of her authority, and so renounced her wedlock (p. 462, ibid.).

Here, the Jewish law is clearly attested to, (for men only), even though Salome chose to appeal to Rome, "her authority."

This is overwhelming evidence. The "toning down" of the command to give a writing of divorce in Deut. 24 in the Revised Standard Version and later translations could be a conscious or unconscious effort to harmonize that passage with that Matt. 5:32 mistranslation of *apoluo* to say "divorced"; and a consequent reluctance to see Deut. 24 command it, even though Jesus called that law a command. A translator's tradition always affects his translation.

A modern translation which does recognize this distinction between *apoluo* and *apostasion* is Eerdman's *The New Testament, An Expanded Translation* by Moody Bible School Professor, Kenneth S. Wuest. In it, Wuest always translates *apoluo* "dismiss" or "put away," and in every case makes the same necessary distinction made by the corrected American Standard Version between that word and *apostasion*. He consistently translated *apostasion* "divorce." His translation does not say, "Whosoever marries her who has been *divorced,* commits adultery (Matt. 5:32)." Wuest's translation states, "Whosoever marries her who has been *dismissed* commits adultery *(italics mine)."* To the women involved — dismissal — could have been much different than written "divorce" and freedom to marry. *Was* and *is!*

SEVEN

ADULTERY AND THE
SANCTITY OF MARRIAGE

THE TWENTY-FOURTH CHAPTER of Deuteronomy is evidence that, even as God heard the groaning of his people in Egypt and provided deliverance, he also provided deliverance for enslaved women, by means of the gift of that tragic necessity, divorce; deliverance in the form of real, written divorce. At least, this appears to be the intent of the law. It says "She may go and be another man's wife."

Surely divorce was never God's ideal. Divorce was his gracious gift to suffering women in a male-dominated society. Yet there is no record of any man granting a written divorce in the entire Bible. There are many accounts of men who married more than one wife. But, even if King Solomon did it, that doesn't make it right. Their multiple wives and numerous concubines (Solomon's 300) were blatant affronts to the will of God as affirmed in Christ, and God hasn't changed!

A long-standing tradition says that adultery can be committed only against a man; that when a man takes another man's wife, they commit adultery against her husband, but not against the man's wife. Also, the tradition argues that polygamy is not adultery because it is not against another man, if the additional wife was not already married. A Rabbi informs me, in response to the magazine article mentioned before, that I am clearly off base because it was proper for men to have more than one wife. Didn't Jesus, even then, consider adultery possible *by any spouse* and *against any spouse?* Notice Mark 10:10-12:

10) And in the house his disciples asked him again of the same matter. 11) And he saith unto them, Whosoever shall put away his wife, and marry another, committeth adultery against *her.* 12) And if a woman shall put away her husband, and be married to another, she committeth adultery *(italics mine).*

Jesus put adultery in a non-traditional setting. Before he came, men saw the threat created by adultery to be the adulteration of a man's progeny; that is, a wife who committed adultery made it uncertain that a man's son was his son. This is a catastrophe to anyone, but was especially so to an Old Testament Jew. Many men hoped to live forever through their blood-line, physically, through an unbroken line of male descendants. To deprive a man of this certainty was serious indeed. A faithful wife was essential.

You will remember how Abraham took Hagar, his wife Sarah's servant, as a wife in order to have a son, Ishmael. Abraham had to have a son. He was desperate because he and Sarah were becoming quite old and had none.

Also, many Jewish men held to the hope that the Messiah might come, and how could he be of a man's lineage if he had no son?

In Jesus we know that eternal life does not come through an earthly blood-line, but comes through faith in God as revealed in Christ. It is our relationship with God which is crucial. And in Christ we learn that not only blood-lines, but also *relationships* can be adulterated; that adultery is more than physical, it can be spiritual also, and can occur against anyone with whom we have a significant relationship.

Even in the Old Testament this can be seen, for God pleaded with Israel about her adultery with other gods. It was for her unrepentant adultery that he divorced her (Jer. 3).

Jesus taught that our *relationships* must be unadulterated. He said, "That whosoever looketh on a woman to lust after her hath committed adultery with her already in his heart (Matt. 5:28)." We should note that this text is part of the major text of this study, Matt. 5:27-32. We are talking about broken relationships, not just laws!

Before Christ came, Jewish men felt that everything was at stake in their sons. As a consequence, through the years, women became, basically, essential instruments to the end that a man have sons, and sadly, to many of them, some were little more than *that.*

Through Christ we see that purity of the relationship of one man with one woman is more important even than whether or not a man has a son. A man can live forever without a son, but not without a pure heart before God.

In this same Matthew 5:27-32, note that the subject of putting away (v. 31-32) is set in the context of warning about adultery (verses 27-30):

> 27) Ye have heard that it was said by them of old time, Thou shalt not commit adultery: 28) But I say unto you, that whosoever looketh on a woman to lust after her hath committed adultery with her already in his heart. 29) And if thy right eye offend thee, pluck it out, and cast it from thee: for it is profitable for thee that one of thy members should perish, and not that thy whole body should be cast into hell. 30) And if thy right hand offend thee, cut it off, and cast it from thee; for it is profitable for thee that one of thy members should perish, and not that thy whole body should be cast into hell. 31) It hath been said, Whosoever shall put away his wife, let him give her a writing of divorcement: 32) But I say unto you, That whosoever shall put away his wife, saving for the cause of fornication, causeth her to commit adultery: and whosoever shall marry her that is divorced committeth adultery (Matt. 5:27-32 KJV). ("divorced" is corrected to "put away" in ASV.)

The only divorce in the Bible (Jeremiah 3:8) occurred because of the unrepentant adultery of Israel, going after other gods. God would not accept this if Israel was to be his. There could be no oneness of spirit. He divorced her. He had to break it up!

And so it must be. When participants in a relationship *cannot* break that relationship, then the chains of slavery have replaced love as the bond that holds them together. The more important the relationship, the more essential it is that either party have the right to break the relationship. This is a spiritual truth. Love must be free.

God did not stop Israel from choosing to leave him. But he *did* give her a writing of divorcement.

The personal relationship we have with God through Christ is of our own free choice. If it were not, a relationship of love could not exist.

Carol Travis, in an article from the *Los Angeles Times,* reprinted in the *Cedar Rapids Gazette,* November 8, 1989, hit the nail squarely on the head when she wrote, "In societies that take marriage most seriously, the divorce rate is highest, because people must have a way out of their most important commitments." These are hard words, but true.

The word "commitment" loses its meaning without the ability to break it. Relationships, which result from commitments of faith, are the most precious things in life. But any relationship is utterly destroyed, and becomes imprisonment if it is not kept by free choice. If my wife were forced to marry me, and were forced to remain married to me, how could I ever know she really loved me?

Marriage has always been the model of relationships in God's dealings with mankind. It described his relationship with his people Israel, and his church, the New Israel. Early on, he declared that it was a relationship of love and trust, not of master and slave, and so a provision for a way out was provided, a writing of divorcement.

Concerning adultery, God insists that we have no other gods before him. He considers his people to be to him a bride. For his people to chase after other gods, to embrace them, is spiritual adultery. To still claim God as our God and yet push him aside and continually embrace others is spiritual polygamy. God would not accept that from Israel, he would not allow himself to be treated as one "put away." He told Judah, "I did not tolerate this with Israel, and will not with you-" Then he recounted what Israel had done, and how he divorced her *(Keriythuwth),* and put her away *(Shalach).*

> And I saw, when for all the causes whereby backsliding Israel committed adultery I had put her away, and given her a bill of divorce; yet her treacherous sister Judah feared not, but went and played the harlot also (Jer. 3:8).

Israel's relationship with God was corrupted. He did not merely turn his back on her and choose another nation, He did not keep her. God said, I divorced her. He literally cut her off and sent her out. Judah, be warned!

In this same Matthew 5:27-31, Jesus also warns us of the ease with which we can become adulterers, and that it is not merely a matter of the flesh, but of the mind; "Looketh upon a woman to lust after her (Matt. 5:28)."

Now, is that all there is to it? NO! Notice verses 29 and 30:

> 29) And if thy right eye offend thee, pluck it out, and cast it from thee: for it is profitable for thee that one of thy members should perish, and not that thy whole body should be cast into hell. 30) And if thy right hand offend thee, cut it off and cast it from thee; for it is profitable for thee that one of thy members should perish, and not that thy whole body should be cast into hell (Matt. 5:29-30).

This is part of that same "put away" passage. Relationships are life and death. Certainly he is speaking here of spiritual matters as well as marital, but Paul tells us in Ephesians 5:25-32 that it is a great mystery, and you can't really separate the two.

> 31) For this cause shall a man leave his father and mother, and shall be joined unto his wife,

and they two shall be one flesh. 32) This is a great mystery: but I speak concerning Christ and the church (Eph. 5:31-32).

Jesus said, you are asking for destruction with your lust. If you put that woman away, and marry another, you commit adultery. You can't have another and keep her.

Then: "If you put her away (without a writing of divorcement) you cause her to commit adultery (Matt. 5:32)." She is *garash,* thrust out. What can she do? Be a prostitute? While still legally married to you? That would be adultery. The penalty for that is stoning (Deut. 22:22). Marry another? While still married to you? That, too, would be adultery. She is still married to you! The penalty, again, is stoning. And it's your fault.

God was willing to forgive even adultery if Israel would only truly repent and love him as her only God. "And I said after she had done all these things, 'Turn unto me.' But she returned not (Jer. 3:7)." So notice that adultery did not demand divorce, though it did justify it. God wanted to relent, if Israel would only repent. As I discuss in a later chapter, forgiveness is allowed. But Israel took other gods, persistently forsaking the true God. For this he divorced her. God pleads for repentance. Forgiveness is possible.

If a person is guilty and is to be punished for adultery, the punishment prescribed by law is not divorce. It is much more severe, for either a man or a woman, "If a man be found lying with a woman married to an husband, then they shall both of them die, both the man that lay with the woman, and the woman: so shall thou put away evil from Israel (Deut. 22:22)."

It seems, by God's own example, that in marriage, as in our relationship with him, he says, "Let your yes be yes, and your no be no (See Matt. 5:33-37)." He is a loving God, willing to forgive, even adultery, but he will not tolerate *unrepentant* adultery. Divorce was God's choice.

Sin is sin. True repentance is the only key. Without repentance, adultery cannot be forgiven, and it brings forth sins just rewards. God was heart-broken. Israel deserved death. He divorced her. He would not keep her in a broken relationship. He chose even divorce to an irrevocably broken relationship or death.

We live in a totally different world than that ancient world, but one to which the same truths apply. We must learn to capture the mind of Christ without being bound by the traditions to which he came. Paul said, "Let this mind be in you which was also in Christ Jesus (Philippians 2:5)."

As opposed to New Testament days, consider: Most of us are not converts from Judaism. Most of us are *not* illiterate. Most of us are *not* farmers, fishermen or shepherds. Most of us do *not* grant special rights of inheritance and authority to the first-born son. Most of us do *not* demand that women be subservient and remain silent in the presence of other men. Most of us do *not* have more than one wife. Most of us do *not* own slaves. Most of us do *not* live in a nation ruled by another nation. Most of us are *not* taught as children to hope to be parents of the long-awaited Messiah. Most of us are *not* totally devoid of any medical understanding or medical terminology. Most of us would *not* insist that only the husband could be the injured party in the case of marital infidelity. We are *not* bound by those traditions. We are free to think, pray, and be guided by the Holy Spirit.

We must take Christ seriously. He changed things. He left us the promise of his spirit. We must take to our traditions his actions, words, context, and motives. Then we must do what he would do, using all the knowledge and resources he has given us, guided by the Holy Spirit he has given us.

The sanctity of marriage is always foremost in the mind of Christ. In Matthew 19 the Gospel writer puts divorce in this context.

> 3) The Pharisees also came unto him, tempting him, and saying unto him, Is it lawful for a man to put away his wife for every cause? 4) And he answered and said unto them, Have ye not read, that he which made them at the beginning made them male and female, 5) And said, For this

cause shall a man leave father and mother, and shall cleave to his wife: and they twain shall be one flesh? 6) Wherefore they are no more twain, but one flesh. What therefore God hath joined together, let not man put asunder. 7) They say unto him, Why did Moses then command to give a writing of divorcement, and to put her away? 8) He saith unto them, Moses because of the hardness of your hearts suffered you to put away your wives: but from the beginning it was not so (Matt. 19:3-8).

Sanctity: "One flesh." "Let no man put asunder." No room for divorce in this ideal. You are responsible. Divorce is *your* choice, not God's. Divorce was commanded because of the hardness of hearts. Divorce should never have been necessary. "From the beginning it was not so." It was not God's ideal, but his grace and his love demanded it.

The context of Deuteronomy 24 seems to indicate that this cruel form of divorce, not written, but unilateral and oral divorce was a common practice accepted by men, but not accepted by God.

The law does not list any specific causes a man had to have to permit him to put away his wife, but, on the contrary, lists *only* two circumstances in which he *may not do so.* If a man accused his bride of not being a virgin, and she proved to be so, he could never put her away (Deut. 22:13-19); or if a man raped a virgin, he must marry her and never put her away (Deut. 22:28-29). These two exceptions to the tradition indicate that putting away for just any cause was a generally accepted practice.

It was a tough time for women. The eighth chapter of the Gospel of John tells of a man and woman caught "In the very act of adultery." A group of men brought the woman to the temple in Jerusalem, intending to stone her, and hoping to use her to make trouble for Jesus (John 8:1-11). The bloodthirsty mob obviously had unlimited life or death power over the woman. No one made a charge against the man. The law required that both the man and woman caught in adultery should die (Deut. 22:21-22). So much for women's right.

A writing of divorcement and freedom to marry again would have provided a woman some degree of justice, and hope. Obedience to the law also would have encouraged the practice of monogamous marriage. Ignore the divorce law and you encourage polygamy, which is adultery, and all the evils that go with it. There are even now nations and religious groups that ignore Deut. 24 and practice polygamy (which is still adultery).

So, bottom line: In his reference to the Mosaic divorce law and his out-spoken rejection of "putting away," does Jesus reject legitimate divorce? No. Divorce came from God through the law to provide justice for cruelly dismissed women, restoring to them the basic right to be married. Jesus rejected abandonment and enslavement, just as did the law; but affirmed the right of those abandoned women to be married.

Christ began, and the Christian faith has continued, the trend toward securing and respecting human dignity for women as well as men. Surely Christ did not rescind this smidgen of justice granted women in Deuteronomic Law, the right to receive a divorce from a man who put her out for another wife. And it was not to be merely an *oral* divorce, either, as practiced by some. Not something so flimsy as to allow a man still to play cat and mouse with a woman, but a written divorce. She was not to be lightly sent away, but given in hand a deliberately written divorce; then never taken back (Deut. 24:4). She had a right to be free from the man who rejected her. It was not perfect. It was tragic, yet necessary. H. E. Dana was certainly correct when he said, in *The New Testament World* (Broadman Press, 1937): "When apostolic Christianity faced out toward the world of its day it was confronted with one of the darkest pictures ever presented in human history (p. 232)." Would Christ and his church ever be able to brighten that picture?

EIGHT

"IF IT IS A GIRL, THROW IT AWAY"

IT WAS A CRUEL AGE for women, even from birth. H. E. Dana in *The New Testament World* quotes *The Oxyrynchus Papyrus 744* as recording the following instructions from a soldier-husband to his wife: "If you bear a child, if it is a boy, let it live; if it is a girl, throw it away (p. 212)." Jesus taught in a society which had no concept of rights for women, in which men had sole authority in the home; a society which was accustomed to total male domination.

Joseph considered "putting away" Mary, the mother of Jesus, when he found her to be pregnant. He had the authority to send her back to her father to be stoned. *Strong's Exhaustive Concordance* (Abingdon Press, 1965) lists "to let die" as one meaning of the word; one person with life or death control over another. It is a word with cruel and merciless connotations when applied to the dissolution of a marriage; the man did or did not do it and the wife could do nothing about it.

When speaking of divorce, Jesus minced no words about seeing all of this as the hardness of men's hearts. Examining biblical history, we find a culture in which male hardheartedness toward women had become so commonplace that it went almost unnoticed, and still does, in that tradition. Jesus did *not* ignore it.

The Gospel of Mark also reports Jesus' divorce reference to Deuteronomy 24, "For the hardness of your heart he (Moses) wrote you this precept (Mark 10:5)." Then Mark's account, in 10:2-5, focused upon proper marriage. He reaffirmed that a man should "cleave to," meaning adhere to or join himself permanently to, his wife (Mark 10:6-9).

Later, after going to a house (Mark 10:10), Jesus taught about desertion and adultery. He taught that if a man dismissed *(apoluo)* his wife and married another (without first giving his wife a divorce), he committed adultery. "And he saith unto them, Whosoever shall put away his wife, and marry another, committeth adultery against her (Mark 10:11)." He still had a wife whom he had dismissed. We call it bigamy when a person dismisses, or puts aside a spouse, without divorce, and marries another. Jesus called it adultery, sin for which the punishment under Jewish Law was death (Deut. 22:22)! He said the behavior we call "bigamy" or "polygamy" is adultery, punishable by death.

Note Mark 10:12— "And if a woman shall put away her husband, and be married to another, *she* committeth adultery (KJV)." Mark's Gospel alone contains this. Here we see that the *same rules apply to women* as to men. Jesus saw that women are capable of being hard-hearted, too.

Those hard-hearted men had been ordered to give the wives whom they had deposed a divorce, and thus one chance for survival, the right to be married. This is what divorce was all about: mercy, and human dignity! God wasn't crazy, he was always a God of grace! The right to marry was not a guarantee of future security, but it allowed room for hope.

Women had not yet dreamed of the rights most enjoy now. But from the beginning, when God decreed husband and wife should become one, he established that unique and highest ideal, a marital state, wherein two lives become so intertwined that to love one is to love the other. This ideal became evident to the apostle Paul after Christ had spent a few short years on earth teaching strange ideas, replacing legalisms with tender mercies, and planting seeds in the hearts of men which would bring forth fruits never dreamed of by the pre-messianic Jewish community. Hear the words of a convert from that tradition, in Ephesians 5:28-29, "So ought men to love their wives as their own bodies. He that loveth his wife loveth himself. For no man ever yet hated his own flesh; but nourisheth and cherisheth it, even as the Lord the church." Now *that* was new!

God's will is surely no less than this, that men and women should both enjoy such a marriage partnership. No other relationship provides adequate human companionship. For mankind, it is essential. God made this clear when he mandated that both must still have marriage rights if their marriage fails, guaranteed by a writing of divorce.

Marriage is essential for mankind!

Maybe this is a good time to warn against antisemitism. We're talking about biblical history and biblical times, so the people we are studying are primarily Jewish people. Paul may have called himself, "... among sinners, the chief," but anyone who is at all observant knows that the men of the Jewish nation were not the chief sinners in their treatment of women.

In many other cultures men treated women at least as badly as they were treated in the Old Testament record, and in fact, some do to this very day.

Laws such as our own Civil Rights Law of 1964 became necessary in order to grant basic human rights to people from whom society had deprived them. Divorce was such a law for ancient women then, granting them the basic human right to be married. Men were depriving them of that right.

Divorce became a tragic necessity because of hardhearted men — a paradox, being both tragic and necessary. Tragic, because it ended that which should never end, marriage. Necessary, to protect the victims of those men who did not play life's game according to the rules laid down by their creator.

Marriage was more than a privilege, yes, more than a right, to those women. Marriage could mean the difference between life and death. To be put out could be to receive a sentence of starvation or of a life supported by adultery; and the penalty for adultery was death by stoning.

Divorce provided a corrective for an intolerable situation. It is a privilege which can be, and often is, radically and diabolically abused. Divorce is not a pretty picture in most cases, but to God was better than death for his beloved Israel, and for the women in Israel. Divorce is a gift of God's love.

NINE

"PIONEERS OF THE NEW HUMANITY"

PRETTY SPRING HILL, KANSAS was struck by a deadly tornado about 7:20 p.m. on a spring day, May 20, 1957. That storm left horrible destruction; many were killed and injured; homes were destroyed; cattle were killed; power was out; fences and farm equipment were ruined. There was utter chaos. Something had to be done. The only thing to do was to get right into the mess and go to work. We had to carry dead and injured to the funeral home and convert part of it into a first aid station, remove dangerous power lines, find a generator to provide some light, search the water of a pond for a body, remove four bodies from a car rolled into a ball, care for people in shock, and meet seemingly endless needs. Now, after the sorrow and the rebuilding, Spring Hill is a pretty town again. The scars have healed. But people who cared had to begin where they were *then,* that horrifying night of May 20, 1957.

Christ began his work with hard-hearted men where the problems were *then.* He came right down into the world. Now, men, you may not appreciate the repeated use of the words, "hard-hearted men," but they are the words of Jesus, and describe the reality of the way men treated women in that society. "When the fullness of the time was come, God sent forth his Son . . . (Galatians 4:4)." A trademark of Jesus is that he always began with people where they were. When we read the scriptures, we may assume the people to whom Jesus spoke possessed our attitudes about women, race, slavery, marriage, and divorce. They had no concept of the rights we all enjoy today.

If we think those men had the least notion that God required a man to have only one wife and be true to her as long as he lived, then we have no idea about where Jesus began. Those were *not* "the good old days."

Jesus' disciples were so dumbfounded when he gave them that lecture on marriage in Matthew 19:1-9 they said, "If the case of the man be so with his wife, it is not good to marry (Matt- 19:10)." They were stunned! Their practice of casting aside wives and marrying others had never been challenged. Jesus had only reminded them of their own scripture from Genesis about the permanency of marriage, quoted from their Deuteronomic Law about divorce, and followed that with a warning against desertion and polygamy. It shocked them! They did not live in a world where men acknowledged such obligations to women.

It is difficult for us to be sure we understand what Jesus said, much less, what the disciples understood him to *mean*. For example, look carefully at one phrase from the statement: "That whosoever shall put away his wife, saving for the cause of fornication causeth her to commit adultery (Matt. 5:32)." "Causeth her to commit adultery." How? Frank Stagg, in *The Broadman Bible Commentary* (Broadman Press, 1969) states:

> The Greek text does not justify the translation "causeth her to commit adultery (KJV)." The infinitive is passive *(moicheuthenai),* untranslatable in English. Something like "made adulterous" or "victimized with respect to adultery" approaches the idea. The RSV is little improvement over the KJV here. We know nothing about Jesus which would justify understanding him to say that an innocent wife — is an adulteress because her husband divorces her (Vol. 8, Matt., p. 110).

Now, look at the word translated "fornication" in the King James Version.

This word also appears in the parallel passage in Matt.

19:9 and is translated "unchastity" in The Revised Standard Version (RSV).

Again, let me refer to Dr. Stagg in The Broadman Commentary (ibid.) about this word:

> The word rendered unchastity *(porneiai)* is usually translated "fornication," and it may denote premarital unchastity. Etymologically the term refers to the sale of one's body in sexuality (Vol. 8, Matt., p. 188).

"Premarital unchastity." Jesus could have been referring to that, to a woman who, after her marriage, was discovered to have sold herself sexually, *beforehand!*

The famous "exception clause" found here in Matthew 5:32 and also in Matthew 19:9 is therefore possibly an *exception to the rule* that a man is responsible for his wife's future, in the case of a bride who sold herself sexually before marriage, and is not exclusive justification for giving a divorce. The law, in such a case, Deuteronomy 22:13-21, grants that exception to a man who took a wife, went in to her, found out he had been deceived, and "found her not a maid (Deut. 22:13)." If the evidence is found to be sufficient, she is to be surely "put away," yes, but her husband is *relieved of responsibility for her future.* He may put her away.

> 21) Then they shall bring out the damsel to the door of her father's house, and the men of her city shall stone her with stones that she die: because she hath wrought folly in Israel, to play the whore in her father's house: so shall thou put away evil from Israel (Deut. 22:21).

This could have gone through Joseph's mind when he discovered his espoused wife to be pregnant. Grace came through Joseph, too, didn't it?

Jesus did not hold a husband responsible for a wife who had married deceitfully, having previously practiced whoredom. She and her father were responsible.

Now, let's look at the whole statement again, "That whosoever shall put away his wife, saving for the cause of fornication, causeth her to commit adultery." What if *apoluo* meant what Jesus said, "put away," and not "divorce"; and the word translated "fornication" *(porneias)* is literally translated "sale of one's body," and the word *moicheuthenai* says "one who is victimized adulterously," as Dr. Stagg suggests? You could have understood Jesus to say something like this: "If you abandon *(apoluo)* your wife and marry another you will be causing her to be victimized *(moicheuthenai)* unless she had been a prostitute unknown to you *(porneias)* beforehand. If you (though not legally divorced) marry another, you will commit adultery. If you put away *(apoluo)* your wife (no divorce) you will make her a victim of adultery *(moicheuthenai)* should she marry another (she needs a bill of divorcement). Your wife's welfare is your responsibility!" No wonder they were shocked.

Marriage is sacred. The woman, who came to marriage, having deceived her husband beforehand, is the only wife for whom he is not responsible, should he put her away. There is another who is responsible for her — *her father.*

Those fellows considered themselves "divorced" when they dismissed a woman, and considered marriage over with *if they said so,* paper or not. But the paper does make a difference; it was truly a necessity in the time of Christ.

Though cruelty was probably not the intent, cruel men fell into a pattern whereby they became tyrants who left women devoid of dignity and deprived of human rights. It was simply their tradition.

And the women had no paper, which freed them to marry again. "Before this bill of divorce be given she is not to be permitted to do so," said Josephus who lived *then.* God knew the difference (as do some Jewish women living in America). Accustomed as men were to absolute and unquestioned life and death power over women, it is not surprising that they were shocked at the words of Jesus (Matt. 19:10).

But God has a way of entering into human suffering and slowly, painstakingly bringing order out of chaos. J. B. Phillips described this "way" of God in the continuation of the earlier quotation from *For This Day* when he wrote:

> *Within this chaos* the early Christians, by
> the power of God within them lived lives as sons
> of God, demonstrating purity and honesty, pa-
> tience and genuine love.
>
> They were pioneers of the new humanity.
> They lived by the power of God within them. We
> must do that too. Today. (p. 20) *(italics mine)*

And Phillips is right! In Christ it is a "new humanity."
We are all "new creatures in Christ Jesus (2 Corinthians
5:17)." But to women, that other half of humanity, who for so
long had been relegated to a lower level of existence, it is
indeed a radically "new humanity."

There was certainly much chaos for God to make orderly
in the "Holy Land," if we consider only the chaotic state of
marriage. Imagine a home into which an additional wife could
be brought (or dismissed) at will. To this add slaves, and
even slave wives for the master and older sons. In addition,
throw in a few concubines. What a mess! Cleaning up the
aftermath of one of our worst tornadoes was child's play com-
pared with cleaning up that!

But Jesus began. The men who caught the woman in
adultery (John 8) walked away ashamedly and left her alone
after he spoke to them of their sin. *That* was one woman
who saw Christ bring change.

The woman in Samaria realized that Jesus was the Christ
and led men to believe in him. Yes, a woman. A woman who
was living with her sixth man, and not even legally married.
She was given *unlimited* opportunity to serve Christ. Women
openly supported Jesus in his work. By the time the apostle
Paul had lived out his life, women had become fellow-minis-
ters with him; and that apostle, a "Hebrew of the Hebrews,"
had written "there is neither male nor female (Gal. 3:28)."
"Pioneers of the new humanity." (ibid.)

TEN

WHO MADE YOU MY JUDGE?

GOD IS NOT THROUGH YET. Today, some churches seem to think everything they do ought to be done exactly as some embryo church, beginning in a Jewish synagogue, did it during the time those letters that make up much of our New Testament were being written. Jesus specifically rejected such ideas, teaching that new wine could not be contained in old wineskins.

Christ set precedents which were in total contradiction to standard religious practice of his day. Remember how he came to earth. God called a woman! Recall the amazement of the woman at the well in Samaria (John 4). Jesus, a man and a Jew, spoke to her, a woman and a Samaritan. It just was not done! In addition to talking with her publicly, Jesus made her one of the first of a new kind of priesthood, the priesthood of believers in the Christ. Visualize all the religious tradition he was discarding!

Jewish law allowed only certain qualified male descendants of Levi to inherit the priesthood and be the mediators (priests) between God and man. This *woman* discovered, through her conversation with Jesus, that he was the long-awaited Messiah, the Christ. She immediately took that good news to *men* in her village. She broke the ice for God's Messiah in a community where no Jew was welcome. Those men became believers through her words (John 4:39). She did the work of a true priest. Here, a sinful half-breed from detested Samaria, a woman, the very antithesis of a priest, the furthest any human could be from meeting the Jewish qualifications for a priest, this *woman* became one of the first of that "royal priesthood" (I Peter 2:9) which began under Christ — "And many of the Samaritans of that city believed on him for the saying of the woman ... (John 4:39)." How can we justify policies in our churches which nullify all the life of Jesus revealed about how God works in that episode alone?

Respect for women, in other roles accorded them by Jesus, in addition to roles as wives and mothers, has come, but slowly. Since women's suffrage in this country, more and more opportunities have arisen for women to participate in activities outside the home, which were once the exclusive domain of men.

In a world where women no longer need to bear every child they can between puberty and menopause in order to provide sufficient population, many women are finding meaningful purpose for their lives in careers other than motherhood.

Laws have changed radically since the days of Moses. With respect to women's rights, probably no laws have advanced more than our divorce laws. In fact, there have been complaints voiced in recent years that, especially in matters of alimony and child support, the laws have come to favor women.

The apostle Paul, writer of much of our New Testament, acknowledged the legitimacy of civil law when he wrote, "For there is no power but of God: the powers that be are of God (Rom. 13:1)." The wisdom, power and grace of God have functioned through civil law, producing significant contributions to mankind. Our civil divorce laws ensure basic equality, fairness, and compassion for those whose marriages have failed. The 35,000 Jewish women in America enslaved by their former husbands, who have put them away by civil law, should have a right to demand that their religion be obedient to their religious law and require the men to grant them a writing of divorcement (Deut. 24:1-3). The difficulty is that their tradition does not allow a woman to require a man to do anything, even what their own law says he must do when he puts away a wife.

Many Christians have resorted to civil laws governing divorce and remarriage. Most have done so with difficulty, and only when they felt they had no other option. As a pastor, I have been told, "Pastor, there was nothing else to do." "Nothing else to do," so they resorted to the legal, compassionate solution provided for their problems by civil law. They felt uncomfortable, having done that which their churches did not approve. Yet good God-fearing people did what they knew they had to do.

Should divorce be allowed? Should the church forbid divorce? Are civil divorce laws acceptable to the church?

I think the proper question would be, "Do we play God, or do we mediate his grace?" Our business in the church is not to make moral decisions for people; but rather, it is to bring them to the one who can guide them toward their own proper moral decisions.

If a man steals a loaf of bread to feed his starving child, then years later comes to church with his child and confesses his sin, do we kill the child? Because God has a law against stealing, do we say the child should have died? No! Nor do we discuss the need for the law against stealing. We suffer with the man in the memory of his tragic time. We assure him of God's forgiveness. We mediate God's grace. And we still don't believe in stealing. We rejoice with him that his child is alive, even if that life still exists only because a man stole.

Our business in the church is not to judge whether or not God, civil law or the church should forbid divorce any more than to judge whether God should provide laws against stealing. Marriage is inviolate. So is property. That does not preclude marriage failure any more than it precludes stealing. Everyone does not always obey God's laws. In fact, "All have sinned ... (Romans 3:23)." Our business in the church is to be redemptive to people. The purpose of this study is not to further the debate as to whether or not divorce is to be allowed. God saw a need for it. God even did it! Though contrary to the perfect will of God, marriages end. In our churches we must move from a judgmental attitude about divorce and the divorced to a redemptive attitude toward divorced people. We must mediate God's grace to them.

Neither do we have the right to indulge in the practice of judging which party in a divorce has a "scriptural divorce" according to the "except for adultery" clause, in order that we might decide on their acceptability. Christ receives all degrees of sinners, even Saul (Paul); the "... sinners; of whom I am chief (I Timothy 1:15)."

The more I counsel with troubled couples, the more I am aware that I rarely know the heart of either. I remember so clearly, a few years back, when I was absolutely convinced of the guilt of a certain wife ... until I finally heard, as Paul Harvey says, "The rest of the story."

When we decide who is acceptable or not acceptable for some church office, by judging who is the guilty party in a divorce, or when we decide who can or cannot marry again, based on this "exception clause," we are making judgments that we probably are not qualified to make. For this reason alone, if there were not cultural and etymological reasons to reject our traditional interpretation of what Jesus said, I would be forced to do so. It makes me my brother's judge. Jesus warns against such judgments (Matt. 7). If I judged someone to be unworthy to serve God, or impossible to be called of God, and thereby caused the waste of that person's lifetime of service, and the person was not judged unworthy by God, and indeed was called of God, what a horrible crime I would have committed. If I judged someone unworthy to be married and was instrumental in causing a lifetime of loneliness, and God had really seen the need and made specific provision for that person's right to marry, what an unnecessary tragedy I would have caused. God gives us the right, indeed the command, to forgive everyone (even the divorced). He gives us the right, indeed the command, to judge no one (not even the divorced).

If I was divorced and someone judged me to be unworthy to serve God or to marry again, the only response I could and must make would be, "Who made you my judge?" If God forgives and God calls, who are we to cancel the forgiving and the calling of God? Would you have *then,* long ago, judged that God really called Mary, an unmarried pregnant girl, to bring his salvation to earth? Would you have *then* guessed he would call a woman to the grave to announce the resurrection of Christ?

In mercifully dealing with marital failure, civil law is ahead of the policies of many churches. Yet Christians, as individuals, have provided much of the leadership and influence in bringing this about. It is sad indeed that church policy often lags so far behind in providing understanding and grace for those involved in this tragic necessity, divorce.

Civil laws governing divorce vary from state to state; some generalities are: Divorce is permitted in order to relieve unreasonable hardship, cruelty or indignity. Dismissal without divorce is not permitted. Remarriage is permitted only after a divorce is final. Marriage to anyone who is married, even one in the process of obtaining a divorce, is bigamy or polygamy, and is forbidden. Children must be protected and provided for when marriage is terminated.

Can we honestly interpret the teachings of Jesus to provide less? Aren't these civil laws in keeping with the spirit of mercy seen in the Deuteronomic Law? Would Christ require a person to remain married in a dangerous, cruel or inhuman situation or when abandoned for another? Can we hear him say that God is unwilling to forgive a person who has been divorced, and that he has cancelled his Deuteronomic provision to allow that person the companionship of a mate? Would Jesus say that any person, even one who was guilty of gross sin culminating in divorce, could not repent, be pardoned, and be restored — fully? Can we visualize Jesus condemning someone, because of divorce or remarriage, to a life beyond his help and the support of his church, through excommunication?

We have in the controlled alcoholic a resource for God, a person who can testify to the power of God and the dangers of alcohol. God really does work for good in all things, we say. All things except marriage failure. Here, his hands are tied, Romans 8:28 fails. Former murderers, rapists and drug addicts of all types, including alcohol and tobacco, are expected to become testimonies to the grace and power of God, if they are Christians. They are assumed to be forgiven and useful in his kingdom even if the offense occurred during a time of weakness *after* the person became a Christian, assuming repentance.

"But marriage makes the two one," they say, "and that can be broken only by death, the two are one forever." Such a literal interpretation of scripture is shocking! It is as though they see the connection between man and woman as only physical. A marriage relationship, in the mind of God, is surely also spiritual. The Apostle Paul equates it with the relationship between Christ and his church, a spiritual relationship, above all else.

> 28) So ought men to love their wives as their own bodies. He that loveth his wife loveth himself. 29) For no man ever yet hated his own flesh; but nourisheth and cherisheth it, even as the Lord the church: 30) For we are members of his body, of his flesh, and of his bones. 31) For this cause shall a man leave his father and mother, and shall be joined unto his wife, and they two shall be one flesh. 32) This is a great mystery: but I speak concerning Christ and the church. 33) Nevertheless let every one of you in particular so love his wife even as himself; and the wife see that she reverence her husband (Eph. 5:28-33).

This is real. This is what marriage can and should be. But relationships, tragically, can be broken. It happens every day, between parents and children, brothers and sisters, man and God; yes, and between husbands and wives.

Marriage should be "What God hath joined together," but it is not always so. Too often, marriage is what lust hath joined together. God is not even considered when many people marry today; therefore, many marriages are flawed from the beginning, never having known the *spiritual* relationship of two becoming one.

Divorce is that essential "out" which must be available in this most important relationship, else it would be bondage, slavery. Marriage cannot be really marriage unless an "out" (which we call divorce) is possible.

Divorce is an inevitable consequence of our promiscuous and hedonistic society. When these tragically flawed marriages fail, we, the church, must be there to help the victims find their way. To our shame, we are eons behind in preparing our young people for real God-ordained marriage. The least we can do is minister to those we have failed.

That woman in Samaria was a glaring example of one who had repeatedly missed the mark in marriage. Isn't it great for one like her to come in contact with the Savior? What Jesus did is the kind of thing we can and must do. It was in that account the Lord said, "... the fields; for they are white already to harvest (John 4:35)."

Millions have been labeled "unfit for service" to God and his church by divorce. How effectively they have been excluded by our judgment that they are unfit! Judged, not by the divorce, but by us! God commanded hard-hearted men to write out a letter of divorcement in order to protect the basic human right to be married. The reason he commanded a writing of divorcement has been lost. In church, instead of God's solution to a cruel problem, divorce has come to be seen as the problem.

Our churches must break free from the traditions of the past which make them ineffective to the divorced. Righteousness demands that all who repent and come to Christ be received as the redeemed in his church, regardless of the nature of their past sins. Just as we all, who are sinners saved by grace, have learned some valuable lessons from our past mistakes, so also some of those divorced people have learned some valuable lessons, lessons our youth need to learn before they make the same mistakes.

Some dear people have learned that it takes more than a "macho hunk" and a "gorgeous bride" to make a real marriage. The church will surely be required to account to God for wasting these people and the lessons they have learned.

Jesus did not waste the woman of Samaria; he received her. Maybe God could still call an unlikely candidate, a divorced woman from among us, or a divorced preacher or deacon, to go break the ice for him in one of the difficult communities he would penetrate with the Good News of Christ today. Would you judge God to be capable of doing *that?*

ELEVEN

HOW SERIOUS IS DIVORCE?

IF IT IS TRUE that divorce provided a degree of freedom and fairness for severely mistreated women, long ago, what is the connection between that and divorce as it is practiced today? Under what conditions can we approve it?

First, let us consider the nature of God. Are the laws of God, and are institutions established by him, such as the church and marriage, designed for the welfare of people, or are people created to fulfill the requirements of the laws and institutions of God?

If we believe that being created in the image of God gives people a special position of love and trust above all else on earth, we will assume God made laws and established institutions for their well-being. We will see marriage as a provision of God's love, for the good of people, not some legal pigeon-hole into which they must fit in order to please him. If of this nature, God would place the well-being of people with marital difficulties above *even* the ideal of permanence in the institution of marriage.

When we look to God for help in these matters, if we see his nature as that of a loving father who knows we sin and come short of his glory, but who, solely because of love, upon our true repentance, forgives and restores us, then our attitude about divorce and remarriage will be different than if we see his nature as that of a stern and unbending lawgiver. We will see this loving father God as the giver of a second chance, the one who says "... Neither do I condemn thee: go, and sin no more (John 8:11)." He will not be the one who, before allowing a marriage to end, would force destruction upon us, demanding we continue in it after it has failed.

We must seek the perfect will of God. This brings us the greatest good and honors God. But because God is gracious, he forgives and picks up and restores to fellowship and usefulness those of us who find ourselves coming short of his perfect will.

We cannot find a *direct* answer in the Bible for meeting many of the needs people have today. We *can* find the mind of God, though. I don't find a diesel engine fuel injector mentioned in the Bible. Still, a man can manufacture, sell, buy, use and repair fuel injectors as he lives in accordance with the will of God, as taught in scripture.

Cultural influences in our society, such as television, the mobility and thus the rootlessness of our people, available leisure time, employment practices, open discussion of intimate personal matters in media, all these and more, are a part of what the church must cope with in order to help people find God's will for their lives. When divorce is socially acceptable and *misused, as it is* now, we in the church have a real challenge in ministering God's grace to the divorced person with love, while maintaining God's standard for marriage. We must do *both!* It is hard to want to minister to people we know have blatantly ignored God's will all their lives in such sacred matters as marriage and family.

In some ways we've come a long way since Jesus responded to a group of rude and self-righteous Pharisees in Palestine. Legal divorce is common now, so common it has become even more of a tragedy. Every divorce represents at least two people whose hopes have been shattered, and there are a lot of them! Dismissal without divorce is less common now, though we still have some of those hard-hearted ones who desert spouse and children, unconcerned for their welfare. Modern divorce legislation does *demand* fairness for the spouse and children. Yet divorce is still no less than a tragedy in most cases, especially for the children.

Deuteronomy 24 requires total separation in divorce, the breaking of all ties permanently. This is extremely difficult when support payments, child visitation, and other events demand a certain amount of contact. These may be necessary and good, yet for many they keep re-opening old wounds and disrupting the healing process.

For some, divorce is more traumatic than the death of a mate. Grief following the death of a spouse is difficult to bear, as is grief resulting from divorce. But the dead spouse does not keep coming back. The divorced one often does, thus prolonging and often renewing grief.

One divorcee said, "Just when I thought he was gone, he popped up again."

Another said, "The separating never totally ends, it's a living hell. It's like a funeral that keeps happening over and over again. He keeps coming back into my life."

Divorce is better than the polygamy or hard-hearted dismissal spoken to by Deuteronomic Law, yet may be the beginning of a difficult life. Anticipated marriage may fail to materialize, and if it does, may be less than ideal. Fear of another marital failure may haunt a person and stand in the way of successful subsequent marriage.

Children are a special concern.

In *Malachi: Rekindling the Fires of Faith,* Dr. Page Kelley writes:

> Recent studies for the effects of divorce on children have shown that in divorce, children always suffer. They are the victims who are hurt most severely.
>
> Some of the symptoms that have been observed in children of divorced parents are these:
> 1. a high incidence of depression and sadness
> 2. guilt over the divorce and an uneasy feeling that they may have caused it
> 3. a refusal to accept the finality of the divorce and a clinging to the hope that the parents will reconcile
> 4. bodily pains and distress
> 5. a tendency to exhibit attention-getting behavior that clashes with the rules of society—

truancy, running away, delinquency, poor school performance, sexual misbehavior, drug use, temper tantrums, and aggression
6. difficulty in resolving normal childhood and adolescent conflicts
7. a tendency to withdraw into one's own private world
8. a fear of forming relationships of intimacy and trust, lest they be hurt again
9. fear of abandonment
10. hurt and disappointment that their parents did not love them enough to stay together
11. a fear of their own failure as marriage partners

A husband and a wife who are marriage counselors tell about a brother and a sister who appeared together in juvenile court, each charged with habitual truancy from school. Each had a lawyer and a supervising probation officer seated nearby. The presiding judge convened the court and asked if the children's parents were present. One of the probation officers explained that their parents had been notified but that they were divorced. Notices had been sent to them, but they had been too busy to come to this or to the previous hearing.

The two children were on the verge of tears, for despite the lawyers' and the probation officers' presence, they felt that no one cared what happened to them. They felt unloved, abandoned and alone.

The counselors said this about the probable future of these two children: "The major victim of divorce is the child. If a prediction were to be made on the future of the two children described above, it would be that the girl might continue a pattern of truancy, drop out of school ... develop sexual relationships on a casual level ... to get the feeling of love that was lacking at home. She may marry while still a teenager ... have one or more children in order to be needed and ... view life as a drudgery ... see herself as a 'nobody' because, after all, she was not worth very much or her parents would have cared ...

"The boy might continue a pattern of truancy, be caught stealing a car in which he is joyriding, be sent to Juvenile Hall repeatedly, and leave school untrained, to go from job to job without steady employment. He may take drugs to feel a part of his peer group, commit petty thefts or burglaries, and end up in the county jail. With a criminal record, his jobs will be only an unskilled type. He may marry while still a teenager, have children at an early age, and view his children as 'nobodies,' just as he was viewed." *(Malachi: Rekindling the Fires of Faith,* Page H. Kelley, 1986 Convention Press, Nashville, Tn., pp. 62-63).

Divorce must not be lightly recommended. The total welfare of all those involved must be considered. Children of the divorced are *always* a special problem. In its proper perspective, divorce is still *only* what it was in Jesus' day, a partial solution to a serious and cruel situation. Yet, as then, it may be the only reasonable solution. Though it may be necessary, *it is always a tragedy!*

Some states have shifted to a non-adversary form of dissolution of marriage. This system does not require one party to prove the guilt of the other. It allows for peaceful dissolution if there is no hope for reconciliation.

Some label this solution "easy divorce" and condemn it. It *does* include the danger of being too easy. Divorce for just any cause, even though legal, and available to either man or woman, is still the same abomination it always was. But if a marriage has failed, there may be a real need for uncontested divorce. A legal battle is not likely to save a marriage. Nor is a judgment of "guilty" necessarily true. There are many people in the state of New York who have agreed to be "guilty of adultery" in order to satisfy the divorce law. In cases where children are involved, court battles and the subsequent public exposure of personal failings may produce further alienation of the parents, and even worse, could do immeasurable harm to children.

Marriage failure comes first, then divorce. That is what the church must see and address. We cannot judge the propriety of the divorce or the guilt of the parties. We mediate grace. It might be possible to prevent some divorces by means of legislative tightening of divorce laws or by religious prohibitions against it, but it is doubtful if such actions will ever restore broken marriages.

When couples stay together only because of fear of the notoriety required by divorce laws, or because of church prohibitions, or "for the sake of the children," tragedy can result. Disastrous marital triangles, domestic cruelty, child abuse, warped personality, murder, and suicide are some of the documented consequences of marriages, which *had failed* but were not terminated. This is reality! What a fearful choice!

In the book by Dr. Kelley previously cited, he quarrels with the Targum, an ancient Aramaic paraphrase of the old Testament, where, in the King James Version Malachi states "God hates putting away," reads: "If thou hate her, give her a divorce." He notes the Greek and Latin versions agree. Dr. Kelley contends that they *mean* "God hates divorce," and also that Josephus was merely succumbing to the standards of the "common fold" when he paraphrased Deuteronomy 24 with,

> He that desires to be divorced from his wife for any cause whatsoever, (and many such causes happen among men), let him in writing give assurance that he will never use her as his wife any more; for by this means she may be at liberty to marry another husband (ibid. pp 50-51).

Normally, I would not argue with such a true scholar and Christian gentleman (and my former Hebrew teacher) as Dr. Kelley. I do, on general principles, agree with him that God hates divorce. He certainly hated his own divorce from Israel. But God hated something else even more. I would state that if God hates divorce, he truly despises what those men were doing in taking additional wives *without* divorce; and I believe, in light of Deut. 24:1-4, that although God hates divorce, things could be bad enough that he could tell a man who hates his wife to give her a writing of divorcement. Marriage is such a sacred privilege that it appears God would remove a person from the clutches of an adulterous tyrant and, by means of a writing of divorcement, restore to that person the sacred right to be married.

A broken home is a tragedy, but I will never forget a young man who put a gun in his mouth and blew off the top of his head, his alternative to divorce. I know that family. That home was broken, too! It was a senseless tragedy, *thanks to heartless advice* from a clergyman who absolutely forbade divorce on threat of ex-communication for him, his wife, and children. The sister of this man asked me, please, to include this experience in my study. If I can prevent even one such tragedy through this study, the time will be well spent, and a thousand times over. Which tragedy do you choose?

If God has within his loving nature the will to give us a second chance, then a lady I know who was divorced "way back when" and has since married a good man — but is guilt-ridden because at church they say she is "living in sin" — must be given, along with her husband, the love and support of a church family instead of criticism and scorn.

Or another, Claudette, a woman in her late thirties. She lives in the same house with Bob, whom she married twenty years ago while still in high school. They rarely speak. Bob's business and social life are "none of her affair." He is cruel, and on rare occasions he expects her to submit to him sexually, solely for his brute pleasure. He does not even attempt to hide his extra-marital affairs. He has broken their oneness. Yet divorce is forbidden by her church, and she is convinced that if she divorced him she could never marry again. She has no "out." She has no marriage, either. She is a brutalized slave. Her only choices are either to live a lonely life of humiliation and cruelty with Bob or a lonely life of guilt without him. Is loneliness, guilt and submission to cruelty God's will for her life? Could anyone need a loving church family more than Claudette?

I have fond memories of a fellow we'll call Jake. As joyous and happy a Christian as you will ever find, the husband of a lovely wife, and the father of children anyone should be proud of. They are a pleasant family and faithful workers in their church — but tainted. When he was sixteen, his fifteen-year-old girl friend became pregnant. They had to get married, but soon were divorced. Now, that is ancient history. But the past is not past at church. He can hold no office there. At church, he and the mother of his children are often subtly (and occasionally openly) reminded that they are "living in sin." Oh, that our churches were filled with families such as that one! That family and the young suicide, above all others, have caused me to ponder this matter day and night.

Ministers are not exempt from marital problems. Men and women who are called to be God's spokespersons and ministers make mistakes, even mistakes involving the choice of a mate. Gary, a young man in seminary, divorced his wife because she left him and was living with another man. "Divorced" is on his record. Will he ever be ordained? Will a church consider him worthy to be its pastor? Can he ever marry? Did God arbitrarily *take away* his right to be married because his wife sinned, or did God *preserve* his right to be married by commanding a writing of divorcement be given when marriage fails? Could God have really called *him?* Or was his call cancelled by his wife's sin? Surely it is obvious that the sin is not in the divorce, but in the behavior that has destroyed the marital relationship.

A pastor in Kansas could not help feeling relief that his daughter had escaped a brutal and dangerous marriage by divorce. He gave serious consideration to leaving the ministry because of the conflict between his honest feeling of relief about his daughter and his life-long teaching that divorce is strictly forbidden.

Pity the pastor of a church whose marriage is dead, but who must maintain a front for the sake of his congregation. His career is doomed and his livelihood is at stake if he considers divorce. What can he do?

Jesus openly ministered to all who came to him. Yet so many of the divorced are afraid of our churches. Yes, *afraid of us!* They know what we *say* the Bible teaches about divorce. Can we be both right and so un-Christ-like? They know that even repentance makes no difference to us; they are still "divorced." The tragedy cannot be undone, yet they need the church. A growing portion of every community has been touched by divorce. We must correct our theology to conform to the life of Christ. We must help them see that grace and truth did come by Jesus Christ. Surely the Holy Spirit will not allow us to continue to say he said one thing and did another. Maybe our mistake was not the mistranslation of *apoluo* in 1611, even though the publishers admitted and corrected it. We have made one somewhere! It's time we found it.

Failure to challenge the traditions of the churches may not have been too serious when divorce affected only a limited number in the past. Maybe then the churches could afford to write them off. I do not think so.

I believe the church has clung to some long-standing errors in translation and interpretation of the scripture, errors which for centuries have excluded from fellowship and usefulness, from joy and equality, even from salvation, many for whom Christ died. Anything, which excludes people from God's grace, is sin! It is time to do something! I think God *wants us* to do something!

TWELVE

WHAT ABOUT IT, PAUL?

WHAT ABOUT IT, Paul? What about us single people? Should we even marry, with the rules as strict as Jesus said?

What about me? I'm already married, but I'm constantly torn between my allegiance to Christ and my home! What about my wife? Do I still concern myself about her, or do I just concentrate on serving God? Should I divorce her so I can totally devote my life to Christ?

What about people who are not Christians? What about a man whose wife doesn't believe? Should he leave her? What about a woman whose husband does not? What can a woman do? What if we separate because of conflict over Christ??? These were real questions, strange as some may seem, to which the apostle Paul responded in these passages of First Corinthians, chapter seven.

> Now concerning the things whereof ye wrote unto me: It is good for a man not to touch a woman. 2) Nevertheless, to avoid fornication, let every man have his own wife, and let every woman have her own husband. 3) Let the husband render unto the wife due benevolence: and likewise also the wife unto the husband. 4) The wife hath no power of her own body, but the husband: and likewise also the husband hath not power of his own body, but the wife. 5) Defraud ye not one the other, except it be with consent for a time, that ye may give yourselves to fasting and prayer; and come together again, that Satan tempt you not for your

incontinency. 6) But I speak this by permission, and not of commandment. 7) For I would that all men were even as I myself. But every man hath his proper gift of God, one after this manner, and another after that. 8) I say therefore to the unmarried and widows, It is good for them if they abide even as I. 9) But if they cannot contain, let them marry: for it is better to marry than to burn. 10) And unto the married I command, yet not I, but the Lord, Let not the wife depart from her husband: 11) But and if she depart, let her remain unmarried, or be reconciled to her husband: and let not the husband put away his wife. 12) But to the rest speak I, not the Lord: if any brother hath a wife that believeth not, and she be pleased to dwell with him, let him not put her away. 13) And the woman which hath an husband that believeth not, and if he be pleased to dwell with her, let her not leave him. 14) For the unbelieving husband is sanctified by the wife, and the unbelieving wife is sanctified by the husband: else were your children unclean; but now are they holy. 15) But if the unbelieving depart, let him depart. A brother or a sister is not under bondage in such cases: but God hath called us to peace. 16) For what knowest thou, 0 wife, whether thou shalt save thy husband? or how knowest thou, 0 man, whether thou shalt save thy wife? 17) But as God hath distributed to every man, as the Lord hath called every one, so let him walk. And so ordain I in all churches (I Corinthians 7:1-17).

25) Now concerning virgins I have no commandment of the Lord: yet I give my judgment, as one that hath obtained mercy of the Lord to be faithful. 26) I suppose therefore that this is good for the present distress, I say, that it is good for a

man so to be. 27) Art thou bound unto a wife? seek not to be loosed. Art thou loosed from a wife? seek not a wife. 28) But and if thou marry, thou hast not sinned; and if a virgin marry, she hath not sinned. Nevertheless such shall have trouble in the flesh: but I spare you (I Corinthians. 7:25-28).

32) But I would have you without carefulness. He that is unmarried careth for the things that belong to the Lord, how he may please the Lord: 33) But he that is married careth for the things that are of the world, how he may please his wife. 34) There is difference also between a wife and a virgin. The unmarried woman careth for the things of the Lord, that she may be holy both in body and in spirit: but she that is married careth for the things of the world, how she may please her husband. 35) And this I speak for your own profit; not that I may cast a snare upon you, but for that which is comely, and that ye may attend upon the Lord without distraction. 36) But if any man think that he behaveth himself uncomely toward his virgin, if she pass the flower of her age, and need so require, let him do what he will, he sinneth not: let them marry. 37) Nevertheless he that standeth steadfast in his heart, having no necessity, but hath power over his own will, and hath so decreed in his heart that he will keep his virgin, doeth well. 38) So then he that giveth her in marriage doeth well; but he that giveth her not in marriage doeth better. 39) The wife is bound by the law as long as her husband liveth; but if her husband be dead, she is at liberty to be married to whom she will; only in the Lord. 40) But she is happier if she so abide, after my judgment: and I think also that I have the Spirit of God (I Corinthians 7:32-40).

Primarily, in the heart of the passage, Paul's message to the Christians was, "Christ made it very clear, and I repeat, 'marriage is sacred:' "

> 10) And unto the married I command, yet not I, but the Lord, let not the wife depart from her husband: 11) But and if she depart, let her remain unmarried, or be reconciled to her husband: and let not the husband put away his wife (I Cor. 7:10-11).

Also, you who are married must remember, that though you are Christians, you are still human, with real desires, real needs, and subject to real temptations. So keep your marriages strong, and true, and fulfilling (v. 2).

Neither cheat on your wife, nor cheat her out of the devotion and the marital fulfillment which are rightfully hers (v. 3-5). If you must be separated because of your devotion to Christ, have an understanding with your spouse beforehand. Don't be presumptuous about your marriage! It, too, is sacred.

And if you are not married, why not just serve God and be patient until the coming of the Lord (v. 7-9, 27). Paul expected the Lord to return any day. He wrote at some length about serving God fully now, without delay, accepting ourselves as we are, content with what we have.

Paul is quite insistent on some matters, such as the sanctity of marriage, "I command, yet not I, but the Lord (v. 10)." On other matters, he only advises. Between the advice about depriving one another of marital privileges (v. 2-5), and the advice to the single not to marry (v. 7-9) he inserts, "But I speak this by permission, and not of commandment (v. 6)."

Writing about "the rest," (v. 12) he was probably counseling them about non-Christians and those others whose marriages included a Christian and a non-believer. In verses 12 and 13 we feel, with him, that Christianity is a serious matter and some non-believing spouses may not tolerate it or those of us who practice it, as was the case with my seminary roommate's wife, and also a pastor friend's professional career-oriented wife. They may leave. We Christians do not (v. 12-13).

If they go, let them go. God has called us to peace (v.15). We are no longer responsible. Should we divorce the one who has left? He doesn't say. The law does say. And he tells us that as long as that mate lives we are to obey the law (v. 39). If indeed our spouse has put us away, the law provides for divorce (Deut. 24:1-4). But, according to Paul, the preferable way would be to remain as we are (v. 27), serving the Lord, praying for reconciliation (v.11) unless he or she marries another. In that case, being obedient to the law, we could never take him or her back (Deut. 24:3-4).

The true burden of the believer with the unbelieving spouse is the salvation of that spouse and the children (v. 14-16). God has set us apart (sanctified) for their salvation. We mediate grace.

If we insist on marriage? O.K. We could make a worse choice, he says (v. 9, v. 28). But remember, time is short. God has much for us to do. Beware of the entanglements of this world. Paul is not dogmatic in most of this. In verse 12 he says, "To the rest speak I, not the Lord." In verse 25 he says, "Now concerning virgins I have no commandment of the Lord: yet I give my judgment, as one that hath obtained mercy of the Lord to be faithful."

In it all, he leaves us with the responsibility to rely upon the guidance of the Holy Spirit. Basically, he gives us this: (1) Marriage is sacred; (2) As long as a separated spouse lives, the law (Deut. 24) applies (v. 39); (3) A spouse might leave a Christian, and if so, that is the departed spouse's responsibility (v. 15); (4) we are set aside for the salvation of our families (v. 12-16); (5) We are called to live in peace (v. 15b); (6) We are not the judge of our brother, but are responsible to God for who we are and what we are given, "But as God hath distributed to every man, as the Lord hath called everyone, so let him walk. And so I ordain in all the churches (v. 17)."

It might be well for all of us to remember that as Christians we have been given the Holy Spirit, and that we should judge ourselves, and not others. In the midst of Paul's letter of instruction to that church at Corinth, a church in turmoil, divided over everything (gifts, the Lord's supper, length of hair, even love); to them, in chapter 11, verse 16, he said, "But if any man be contentious, we have no such custom, neither the churches of God."

Could we possibly start over again in our relationships, with our personal prejudices and our traditions replaced by the Spirit of Christ to guide us? Could we trust Him that much?

THIRTEEN

DIVORCE IS NOT THE PROBLEM

THE SAVING GRACE of God in Christ is available to recreate us, to change us; to remove our "hardness of heart" and thereby redeem us from such evils as polygamy, infidelity, exploitation, and cruelty. Redemption in Christ should enable God's original plan for marriage (repeated by Jesus) to become a reality: that man and woman should truly become one, permanently. If this prevailed we would not need divorce. But there are still some hard-hearted men, and, as hinted by Jesus in the Gospel of Mark, even some hard-hearted women. Some people still need divorce.

We are often reminded of the high divorce rate. It may be necessary for it to go even higher before it can legitimately come down. These may be harsh words, but stay with me. Part of the fault is ours. Divorce is not the basic problem. The problem is that marriages fail. Divorce is the result of marriage failure. That is the real tragedy; marriages fail! A divorce is only the legal instrument which declares that a dead marriage is legally buried. Divorce is the legitimate way out.

The U.S. Navy was not crazy enough to send my two sons into duty in nuclear submarines without serious preparation. You have to be properly prepared in order to successfully complete a tour of duty of 105 days under water, confined with a crew of other people. It is essential that every person know what to expect and how to cope with it, and how to cope with the unexpected. The welfare, and possibly the life of each individual, and the crew depend upon it.

Life has become exceedingly complex. Family life is no longer the simple, isolated, and insulated matter it was just a few years back, in rural America. There are people in every community who are trained to take from any young couple in America their money, their self-respect, their religious faith, their health, their idealism, and even their lives.

There are not only people in real life who will make a couple both sick of themselves and of each other over an insane auto purchase they were conned into, but there are plenty of them who will do the same through their social activities, their children's education, and even their church life.

The whole atmosphere in current life in the United States is a constant barrage of slick advertising designed to drain every last ounce of worth of any kind out of us, and most young couples are in no way prepared to cope with it. And the church is not innocent in this matter. Keep a couple harassed for money and time and then don't be surprised at the report that half of those couples are now coming apart at the seams.

We must wake up to the fact that proper, enduring marriage is essential to the welfare of mankind. Many young people are entering into relationships which have no foundations for becoming good and enduring marriages. As long as our abnormal culture, dominated by television, continues to pressure adolescents into relationships based on sex appeal, and for which they have received no preparation for coping with the realities of married life, the safety valve called divorce will remain a necessary "out" for vast numbers of people God did not join together. We need not bemoan the high divorce rate. We created it. We must see it for what it is, an honest indicator of the vast number of people who enter marriage totally unprepared, even unaware of what marriage can and should be. The real problem is our rate of bad marriages.

This reality demands far more from us than just preaching against divorce! It will be more difficult. Divorce is a phony issue, but is easy to preach against. Approval by our traditional congregations is assured. *It is something else for a church to be constructive in providing preparation for marriage.* It is an exercise in futility for a church to preach against divorce and ignore the problems of faulty preparation for and concepts of marriage. This is what we have done for as long as I can remember. It makes as much sense as if we were to preach against hospital emergency rooms and ignore drunken driving. We preach against the relief for a cruel problem, and ignore the cause of the problem.

Something else is developing which is aggravated by our bad marriage rate. Many young people are choosing a variety of currently popular, but dangerous alternatives to marriage. Because our marital success rate is so low, many young people fear to marry. Our society once assumed that virtually everyone would choose one of two life-styles, singleness or marriage, but that is not so today. Live-ins, contract marriages, common-law marriages, communes, and even homosexual marriages are openly espoused today. The real problem which we must recognize and solve cooperatively at home, school and church is our failure to prepare our young people for the kind of marriage God wills them to have, and motivate them to choose it.

Home! The standard set by our schools and churches is not likely to rise above the moral standards prevailing in our homes; yet, in a vicious cycle, we look to our schools and churches to help us improve our home life. Our schools and churches need good leaders, but the only source for these leaders is our homes. To break this vicious cycle, parents must accept the responsibility of evaluating and *controlling* the things which influence the development of the moral values of their children at home. Busy parents must somehow find time to parent.

The average person in the United States now watches 26 hours of television per week. What do children learn from it? What does it do to them? They watch TV for about the same amount of time they spend in school. This is 26 times as much as is spent in Sunday School if they attend every week. Most don't. What kind of life do they see portrayed here as "normal"? If not, at least, interpreted on the spot as abnormal, how will it affect their lives?

Now that both parents work outside the home in roughly half our families, what are the children learning from the substitute parents who care for them? Who provides that care?

Schools! What do children really learn about marriage at school? Are they taught that those alternate life-styles they see on television which deviate from monogamous marriage or singleness are *not acceptable* life-styles for their own well-being? Will Christians ever consider *public school teaching* a valid Christian calling *on a level* with the importance of *missionaries and pastors?* We have one of the greatest challenges on earth in American *public schools.* I'm not talking about forcing religion *on* our schools; I'm talking about paying the price to be Christian, salt and light *in* our schools.

In order to reduce the need for divorce, we must do it positively, by finding ways to provide better preparation and incentive for proper marriage. In school, our children *may* learn the chemical make-up of their bodies, but they *must* learn about living with a spouse! Some schools have innovative programs to provide specialized training in trades and careers into which students *may* enter. Marriage must be a major consideration for which virtually every student *should* prepare to enter. Here *all* students need extensive and practical instruction. Classes on marriage and family life now offered are likely to be elective and too often are "crip" courses of little substance. The human dynamics involved in marriage are rarely taught.

Young adults are poorly prepared for the responsibilities and crises which develop in a close, exclusive, intimate and long-term relationship such as marriage. Many have never seen a proper relationship at home, and some are taught at school by teachers who do not enjoy healthy marriages. It is not hopeless. More and more people are seeing the problem. But the problem is real and serious.

What training has today's high school dropout mother received to help her understand the jealousy her immature husband suddenly feels because she is giving attention to his own baby son?

How do we help a young couple understand and resist the temptation of alcohol, when it is so professionally promoted in their living room as a necessity for joyous living?

Church! How will those who, if exposed at all, are exposed only to the religion of the "electronic church"-offered up so enticingly by men with pink ruffled shirts and women with low-cut gowns — ever see that this leaves them empty, devoid of commitment to the Lord's body, his church? How can we help them see they are missing the genuine, but costly learning, loving, and sharing relationships of a real local church? How can we communicate to them the sense of purpose and meaning for life which comes from "being" the church?

How can we help millions of youth avoid a "marriage" which shortly ends with a "nothing left" feeling, after a burned out romance based on sexual attraction alone?

Who will teach an over-protected youth who reached age 18 without any responsibility for the welfare of any living thing the way to deal with an unexpected death, a moral lapse, or a relational failure? How many who marry know that all their behavior produces sure and just consequences? Who will prepare them for these things? The schools do not. Someone must! Churches generally are locked in to painting idealistic pictures of marriage which rarely, if ever, exist.

Some of our churches and denominations are beginning to provide some help for the family. Marriage and family enrichment seminars, conferences, and retreats are becoming more common, as are denominational publications which focus on needs of the divorced and singles. Seminaries are providing better training for family ministry. All of this helps, but we are far behind. Most of what we do is a band-aid approach to provide first aid for flawed marriages, after the fact of ill-prepared beginnings. Somehow, we must help youth *prepare* for marriage beforehand. Only a small percentage of those between age 18 and 25 even attend church. High school and college are crucial stages of development where these needs could be met. We must find ways to help.

Marriage is still the ideal, two equal but different people, permanently married, man and wife, for the fulfillment and completeness of both and the proper nurture of children. The most satisfying and rewarding married life ever known is possible today. Living standards are high; housing excels all past history; couples can easily plan their families; excellent medical care is available; most families have ample free time for leisure activities. The kings of Jesus' day could not enjoy recreational facilities equal to those available to even a poor family in the United States today. Now is the best time ever for God's kind of marriage and family life.

As long as people are not motivated and equipped for real marriage, divorce will remain a tragic necessity. A safety valve. When we condemn divorce we do not help those who find themselves trapped in impossible marriages. We can legitimately pray that the divorce rate *will come down* only when we learn how to help young people enter marriage equipped for it with the knowledge, spiritual strength, and emotional stability necessary to make it what it should be.

Let us pray that the divorce rate *does not come down* because more and more fearful and disturbed people avoid marriage and choose alternate and destructive life-styles.

Divorce for just any cause? No! Divorce is serious business, but it was given by God as a humane solution to an intolerable situation, a matter of grace. We live in no utopian millennium now. Perfectly prepared Christian people who know and will always obey the will of God are *not* the only ones who marry. Marriage failure is a grim reality among both Christians and non-Christians. Divorce is still a necessity. God is a God of justice, and a basic sense of justice demands, if marriage fails, that the man and woman are to protect each other by the giving of a divorce. As Moses directed long ago, whether you are right or wrong, if you remove yourself from a marriage, you must free the other person, utterly and completely. God's law *and* man's agree here. Divorce is an instrument given by God through which the basic human right to be married is protected after a marriage has irrevocably failed; a tragic necessity and a precious gift.

FOURTEEN

GOING ON

I WRITE THIS FINAL CHAPTER with the prayer that if you are married, your marriage will continue and be a good marriage, and if you are divorced, you will find real peace: peace with self, peace in the church, peace with God. The Gospel of Jesus Christ is really good news, good news for everyone.

If you are divorced, you may be someone who made a terrible mistake in choosing divorce — and who knows it now, or you may be a teenager who doesn't know for sure what really did happen; or maybe even now you are a grossly unrepentant person who took advantage of another; or a serviceman whose wife found someone else to live with while you were overseas; or a middle-aged pastor's wife whose husband married his secretary; or a pastor; or a deacon. Divorced people are of all races, ages, colors and creeds, both male and female, Christians and non-Christians.

We can't avoid the discussion of sin if we honestly discuss divorce. The two words are sometimes used almost synonymously. To many good people "divorce is sin." Despite this popular notion, they are not the same. Sin may describe the behavior which caused a divorce. If so, it must be dealt with.

Basically, sin consists of failure to live in accordance with the will of God. We have all done that. When our behavior comes short of God's will, it is sin. When we do that which opposes God's will, that is sin also. The Bible teaches that God's standard for marriage is the exclusive commitment of a man and woman to each other for life. Many, for a myriad of reasons, come short of that. Whatever causes the failure of a marriage is sin. If a marriage fails, if reconciliation cannot be attained; then this obviously comes short of God's standard.

Divorce has not yet entered the picture. Divorce is not the sin. The behavior is the sin. Divorce is a legal process into which the marriage partners may enter *in order to deal with marital failure.* Divorce, that final step of ending a marriage, provides fairness for both parties as they go on from the end of a marriage which has been acknowledged to have irrevocably failed. Divorce, in itself, may actually be a gift of God whereby both parties can begin to rebuild their lives. It officially ends that marriage. It was meant to do so (for cast out women) when Deuteronomy 24 was written; and it is a legal procedure which can meet a real need today, the need to officially end a marriage that no longer exists.

Are God's grace, his love, and his care available to the divorced? How do we deal with the behavior, the sin, which caused a marriage failure? God's grace extends to all, but to use Deitrich Bonhoeffer's term, it is not "cheap grace" (*The Cost of Discipleship,* McMillan, 1970).

God's first requirement for forgiveness of sin is honest confession. Did you do wrong? You may have to go all the way back to the decision to marry. All marriages are not made in heaven. Was it wrong from the beginning? If your decision to marry was right in every way, what irrevocable thing has happened? Why? Is it really too late to do anything about it?

If your marriage has failed and you are divorced, the failure is probably not the fault of only one partner. In most cases some of the blame falls on both. God can forgive, but only after honest soul-searching, honest confession, and repentance.

Repentance is turning around; it is a heart-felt desire to turn from any way which is not the will of God. Forgiveness of sin requires that. He doesn't forgive what we keep on doing. We can never be comfortable until we are sure our sin is forgiven, until we admit the whole truth to God, and with all our hearts *turn* and honestly seek his will for our lives.

With true repentance, the failure of a marriage, though tragic, can be forgiven just as other failures to meet God's standards for our lives are forgiven. There are no sins too big for God, if we're honest. Marriage failure is not the unpardonable sin. "If we confess our sins, he is faithful and just to forgive us our sins and to cleanse us of all unrighteousness (I John 1:9)." The good news for divorced people is that this scripture does not exclude what you did to cause your marriage to fail.

What if you are divorced and are convinced that your marriage failure was the fault of your mate or of someone else? Well, somebody caused it, and sooner or later you will have to deal with your feelings about that person. It means forgiving *others*. It is not as difficult for us to accept God's forgiveness of our sins as it is for us to forgive those who sin against us. We are not talking about forgiving someone who cheated you out of five dollars or dented the fender of your new car. We are talking about something most serious and most difficult to forgive, sin which may have destroyed a large portion of your life, and may have hurt other people, including your children.

If your marriage has failed, and you could not prevent it, you are still left with an area of responsibility. You entered into something momentous, a sacred relationship, one which was meant to be exclusive and permanent. Juan, in John Steinbeck's *Wayward Bus* (Viking Press, 1947), thought about leaving his wife, Alice; but he told himself he would not, "Because she can cook beans." Steinbeck went on to say:

> But there was another reason, too. She loved him. She really did. And he knew it. And you can't leave a thing like that. It's a structure and it has architecture, and you can't leave it without tearing off a piece of yourself. So if you want to remain whole, you stay no matter how much you dislike staying.

But what if the unthinkable has happened? "Divorce granted." Somebody didn't stay, but life must go on.

Divorce leaves you with a piece of yourself torn off, no matter how bad the marriage. There has been a physical and mental union which cannot be easily dismissed. You engaged in one of life's most serious relationships, and the most intimate, a marriage relationship with another human. Neither of you will ever be the same. It is a relationship which cannot be cut off without leaving scars. It is possible to live with the scars, even to see them partially heal. You can pick up the pieces and make a new life; but you are part of a serious marriage failure which you must honestly face and for which you *must forgive* any failings before you can have the peace you seek.

If there was no way on earth you could have prevented the failure of your marriage, you must still forgive that person who caused it. That may not sound like very good news. It may not be easy. But you'll never regret it. You will not find peace without it. Jesus said: "If ye forgive men their trespasses, your heavenly father will also forgive you: but if you forgive not men their trespasses, neither will your father forgive your trespasses (Matt. 6:14-15)." Having married someone, you accepted the ultimate human responsibility. If your marriage has failed, in order to find peace, you must forgive your former mate, even if your mate was totally at fault.

I cannot over-state the fact that marriage is sacred. Divorce must be considered only when there is absolutely no marriage left. Not only because marriage is sacred but also because divorce must constitute an *absolute end* to the relationship. Many people flirt with divorce — and thereby flirt with tragedy. The passage in Deuteronomy 24 specifically prohibits taking back a former mate if that previous mate has married another.

Because marriage is sacred, the primary purpose for divorce is to preserve the basic human right for both parties to be married *after* the failure of a marriage has become established. Because this right is specifically the right to marry again, divorce *must be final*. An adulterous marital triangle exists in any subsequent marriage if the previous marriage is not absolutely terminated, *both physically and mentally.* Jesus warned that mental adultery is as sinful as physical adultery. This certainly includes a warning to those who marry after a divorce. No halfway measures will do. You cannot be true in spirit to a new mate while still attached in any sense to one from the past. Divorce must be absolute!

The most tragic divorces I have seen are the ones which were mistakes. Regardless of the reasons for considering a marriage to be finished, if something can be done to restore the relationship, divorce *must not* be considered.

God is willing to help you overcome marital problems. People have overcome seemingly impossible obstacles to successful marriage, have even grown and developed because of them. Out of unbelievable chaos have come some truly beautiful marriages. True repentance and forgiveness work some miracles hard to believe. God has granted to those who would receive it the grace to forgive sins you may not be able to imagine, and has restored some horribly shattered relationships. He is still able and willing. Nothing is impossible with God. Seek him with all your heart!

More than once, while counseling troubled couples, I have been struck with the thought, "What these people really need is to truly marry each other." I mean forsake self, forsake all others, and really give themselves to each other. That's all a lot of couples really need to do to solve their problems.

Interference from family, friends, even church or children, may cause disruption of a relationship. Couples forget that when they became one in marriage they were required to forsake all others — *specifically* their parents. Financial problems are also major sources of marital problems.

Personal and marriage counseling are available. Many churches have well-trained pastors who are willing to help. Counties, states, cities, colleges and hospitals, as well as churches have counseling available at minimal or no cost. By all means, find some help if your marriage is at stake. You have too much to lose!

In conclusion, divorce is a tragic, but legitimate, end to a marriage that is over, once the marriage has irrevocably failed.

Divorce means an end to any hopes that the marriage might be saved, and declares publicly that the marriage has ended.

Divorce began long ago, to provide a degree of human dignity for women living in a cruel age, an age in which they were subjected to cruel dismissal and to the whims of hard-hearted men.

Divorce declares the legal end of a marriage, and thereby precludes against any charge of bigamy or adultery in a future marriage.

Divorce severs all marital ties and all control by the former spouse.

Divorce provides freedom from a former spouse, freedom to live unmolested, and freedom to marry again.

Divorce is a major historical provision for the protection of the first basic human right, marriage. It provided women, who were once arbitrarily dismissed from their marriages for just any cause, the right to again be married. The right to be married is a sacred right.

Divorce remains a social and legal necessity. When marriage has failed, divorce provides a legal and moral place to start again.

Divorce is the aftermath of one of life's worst tragedies, the tragedy of marriage failure. To those who have suffered this, divorce can be a gift of God. If that gift is all you have left from your marriage, accept it, forgive and go on in peace.

So, to sum it up, *we are wrong* when we say Jesus taught that divorce is absolutely not permitted, or at best, is permitted only in the case of admitted or proven adultery. We have seen that extreme circumstances once demanded divorce; they still do.

We are wrong when we interpret Christ to say a divorced person is not allowed to marry again. God commanded divorce in order to preserve the basic human right to be married "... She may go and be another man's wife (Deut. 24:2)."

We are wrong, indeed, when we say Christ taught that a divorced person who does marry again lives in adultery. Of course, those cast out, but *not divorced,* married women of

110

Jesus' day had a problem if they married again. But divorce was not the problem; divorce was the *solution,* ordered by God.

Certainly the apostle Paul was concerned about decent home life for leaders in God's work. But "husband of one wife" was the reason the law demanded divorce. Men of Paul's day did not normally grant legal divorce, but put away their wives and took *additional* wives. Paul was probably *affirming* Deuteronomy 24:1-2, which *limited* a man to one wife. Paul did not (nor do we today) want leaders in the churches who had numerous wives and concubines, even if it was the tradition of the day.

And finally, *we totally miss the mark* when we forbid people to serve Christ, based on whether or not they have been divorced. God calls whom *he* chooses.

Divorce can be the instrument whereby marital chaos may be straightened out. Divorce can be the starting place for a person to have the possibility of a decent marriage as "the husband of one wife," or "the wife of one husband."

Like those men in Galilee, we might be shocked if we really heard the Lord speak to us about marriage and divorce; if we heard him say "marriage is permanent;" if we heard him reiterate "hard-heartedness causes divorce," or "you are responsible for the future of your current spouse." Perhaps many today would shudder, too, and say, "maybe we'd better not even marry." Maybe many shouldn't!

But we must hear Christ say that marriage is sacred and is the right of every person; we must not wrongfully use his teaching to construct barriers between him and any one for whom he died; we must not think that any among us cannot give our lives in service to him.

He might, even now, surprise us by calling a young pregnant Mary, a tough Mary Magdalene, a crude Peter, a murderous Paul, a young Greek Titus, a deaconess Phoebe, or even a five-time loser from Samaria to bring his salvation to our world. Would we allow him to do it in our church? Are we ready to pay the price to be mediators of the grace and truth which truly did come in Jesus Christ?